Peace
in
Jerusalem

But the battle
is not over yet!

CHARLES GARDNER

OlivePress צהר זית

Messianic & Christian Publisher

PEACE in JERUSALEM

But the battle is not over yet!

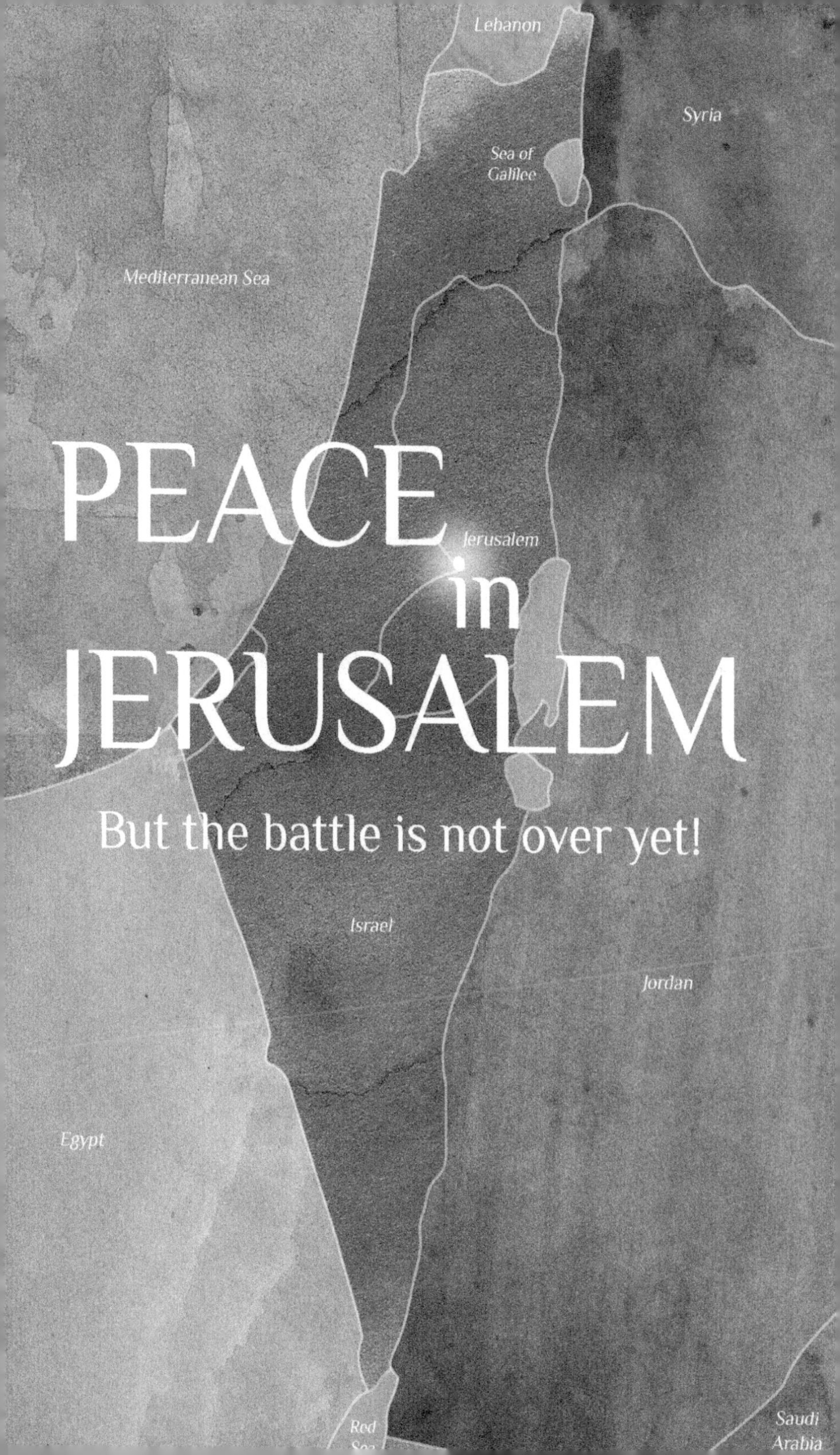

PEACE IN JERUSALEM But the battle is not over yet!
ISBN: 978-1-941173-10-7
Copyright © 2015 by Charles Gardner

Published by
Olive Press Messianic and Christian Publisher
olivepresspublisher.com

Printed in the USA and UK

Messianic & Christian Publisher

Cover design by Karen Keene (karen.keene@gmail.com)
Back cover photos © 2015 by the author
Photos on p. 74 © 2015 by Cheryl Zehr

NOTE: Having a British author and an American publisher, the choice was made to mainly use American grammar and spelling, yet keep some British flavor.

In honor to God all pronouns referring to the Trinity are capitalized; satan's names are not. [Exceptions to this are in Scripture quotes of versions, such as NIV, that do not adhere to this policy.]

Dedicated to my beautiful wife, Linda, out of gratitude for her constant love and support.

And with grateful acknowledgements to the many people who have influenced and inspired me over the years.

Other Books by the Author

Israel the Chosen: Why the Jews are So Special

Tongues of Fire: The Phenomenon that Set the World Alight

Doctor on the Run: The Memoirs and Prescriptions of Dr David Gardner

FOREWORD

This book should cause every reader to examine his heart: Am I part of the church which is asleep to the reality of the centrality of Israel and the Jewish people in the mega-plan of God? Or am I searching the Scriptures diligently to rightly read "the signs of the times"? Have I stood firm in this or have I bought into the predominant cultural bias against Israel which stands against the clear words of the Bible?

In this unique book, Charles Gardner reports on the results of the second *At the Crossroads* conference held at Christ Church, Jerusalem, in May 2014. Rector David Pileggi and his international team had already seen God's miracles displayed at the first of these by-invitation-only conferences held two years earlier which brought 70 leaders to Jerusalem from across the Middle East.

What were the miracles? For a starter, most of the leaders (many of them Muslim-background believers) were coming from countries which do not give diplomatic recognition to Israel! Arranging for entrance visas was impossible for most. But the vision of **Isaiah 19:23-25** had quickened the spirits of David and others in Jerusalem—*"In that day there will be a highway from Egypt to Assyria ... and the Egyptians will worship with the Assyrians. ... Israel will be the third with Egypt and Assyria, a blessing in the midst of the earth, whom the LORD of hosts has blessed, saying, 'Blessed by Egypt my people, and Assyria the work of my hands, and Israel my inheritance'"* (ESV).

And so they set out in faith to do the impossible! They knew God was calling them to be part of this Biblical vision penned by Isaiah over 2,500 years ago! There **would** be a

6

highway which would tie most of the Middle East together in prayer and fellowship. God had spoken!

Charles brings his years of experience and skill as a journalist to record some of the marvels of the 2014 conference. Little did the participants know that a month after they returned to their respective homes, rockets would again rain down on the towns and villages of Israel courtesy of Hamas in Gaza, precipitating the next round of conflict in the Land. Or that ISIS forces would rampage across Iraq and Syria, horrifying the world with their barbarity, and recruiting hundreds of youth to its cause.

The search for peace in the Middle East, Charles rightly concludes, will never be accomplished by politicians and diplomatic bureaucrats. *It can only be achieved by the work of the Sar Shalom, the Prince of Peace, Yeshua/Jesus, who paid the price with His dear blood shed on Calvary in the city He calls His own – Jerusalem.* Only Jesus can reconcile individuals to the Father and, as a result, to one another. By bringing leaders together in Jerusalem to pray, worship, repent of nationalistic pride and racial hatred, tell their stories, and fellowship in their Lord Jesus, the prophecy of Isaiah began to take on flesh!

I met Charles Gardner at Christ Church Guest House on his first visit to Israel in the autumn of 2013 which he chronicles in these pages. Like Charles, I was trained as a journalist; unlike Charles, the 2013 CMJ* Shoresh study tour I had just completed was the most recent of many I had led since 1976.

---

* Church's Ministry Among Jewish People

Using the 2014 *At the Crossroads* conference as a springboard, Charles shares testimonies of God's supernatural power not only in the lives of conference participants but of others who have met Jesus in dramatic ways across the Middle East. His chapters fill in the space of history which brought Israel into being. The author clarifies historical facts which have been revised beyond recognition by the liberal media and politicians of our day. He catalogues the fate of nations which do not take seriously the word of God to Abram: *"I will bless those who bless you, and whoever curses you, I will curse"* (Gen. 12:3).

I am personally grateful to the author for putting into one volume the teachings that we in CMJ have spoken in churches around the world about God's plan for His people, His love for the Jews, and of the centrality of Israel in His eternal purpose. As the first director of CMJ USA in 1980, I can say that it was seldom that I found church people—clergy or lay—enthusiastic about taking the Gospel to their Jewish friends, neighbors, or family members. CMJ's educational work is to change this profile and encourage the Church to do what Scripture calls us to do—to provoke the Jews to jealousy, to pray for their salvation, and to lead them to their loving Messiah. Instead, many hear errant theologies such as "replacement" or "two-covenant" teachings either from pulpits or simply from popular church culture. Charles' book addresses these issues from a Biblical view.

And there is Israel itself. Since its legal establishment in 1948 following the Holocaust, Israel's enemies have refused to recognize her and vow to "drive her into the sea."

The 15 million Jewish people in the world today are seldom having the Gospel preached to them—even though it was sent first to them by a Jewish Messiah and an early all-Jewish church—and, though its life is threatened daily, Israel is off the radar screen for most professing Christians. Charles Gardner puts the challenge before me: Will I be filled with His Spirit and full of His Word like the "wise virgins" of the Gospel parable, or will I be found sleeping in this crucial moment of history as time draws to a close?

Dr. Theresa Newell
Chairman, CMJ USA
Ambridge, Pennsylvania, USA

Peace I leave with you;
my peace I give you.
I do not give to you as the world gives.
Do not let your hearts be troubled
and do not be afraid.
John 14:27

And the peace of God,
which transcends all understanding,
will guard your hearts and your minds
in Christ Jesus.
Philippians 4:7

Pray for the peace of Jerusalem:
"May those who love you be secure. ..."
For the sake of my brothers and friends,
I will say, "Peace be within you."
Psalm 122:6, 8

I will make a covenant of peace with them;
it will be an everlasting covenant.
Ezekiel 37:26a

In that day there will be
a highway
from Egypt to Assyria. ...
The Egyptians and Assyrians will worship together.
In that day
Israel will be the third,
along with Egypt and Assyria,
a blessing on the earth.
The LORD Almighty will bless them, saying,
"Blessed be Egypt my people,
Assyria my handiwork,
and Israel my inheritance."
Isaiah 19:23-25

Nation will not take up sword against nation,
nor will they train for war anymore.
Isaiah 2:4b

Every man will sit
under his own vine and under his own fig tree,
and no one will make them afraid....
Micah 4:4

Table of Contents

1

Dividing Wall of
Hostility Destroyed

As politicians preside over the abject failure of another attempt to resolve the Israeli-Palestinian conflict, and as much of the Middle East is engulfed in flames ignited by Islamic fanatics, what hope is there for peace?

Well, I have witnessed at close hand the answer to the crisis. I have seen with my own eyes Arab and Jew embracing one another in Jerusalem, that beautiful city God calls His own!

In a 40-year career in journalism which has encompassed political struggles in other parts of the globe, and which has also included coverage of some of the world's greatest sporting events, nothing compares with the thrill of what I have recently experienced on Mount Zion.

I love the way Mark Twain introduces his classic *Huckleberry Finn*: "You don't know about me without you have read a book by the name of *The Adventures of Tom Sawyer*." In the same way, you will have learned something about me through a book called *Israel the Chosen*. But in case you haven't, and at the risk of repeating myself, I will re-introduce myself somewhat so that what follows is set more comfortably in context.

My first book on the subject, *Israel the Chosen,* was published shortly after I took early retirement from South Yorkshire Newspapers at the end of 2012, and was the result of hearing the distinct "voice" of God speaking to me thus: "I want you to be a helper of Israel." However, the book was only the beginning. It was as if all those forty years had been a sort of "wilderness" preparing me for my real calling which would only be fulfilled following retirement!

Yes, I have found that He has indeed called me to the Kingdom "for such a time as this," as Queen Esther had been millennia ago when God used her to save her people from destruction.

I found myself in a parish church not far from where I live, in Doncaster, South Yorkshire, listening to representatives of an organization with which I was familiar: the *Church's Ministry Among Jewish People* (CMJ). I learned about an inaugural conference called *At the Crossroads* which had been held at their Jerusalem headquarters at Christ Church the previous year, in 2012, in which Arab Christian pastors and Jewish followers of Jesus (known as Messianic Jews) had met together to seek ways they could further support and encourage one another. The Arabs among them had travelled from all over the Middle East at great risk to their lives (from a Muslim world fiercely opposed both to Judaism and Christianity) and had embraced their Jewish brethren. This wasn't an attempt at reconciliation; they were already reconciled, I was assured.

I had felt my heart "strangely warmed," as it were, on hearing about what had happened at that conference (and seeing something of it on a DVD), rather as John Wesley had described his conversion, and indeed it represented a turning point—a new direction—in my Christian life that now exceeded 40 years. The desire to see reconciliation at work was something that had long been close to my heart: between English and Afrikaner, between black and white in South Africa where I grew up, between Protestants and Catholics in Northern Ireland where my wife, Linda, had worked and prayed to that end for several years, and even between church people who often fell out with each other. I have seen the Holy Spirit moving powerfully in this way, especially during meetings in Sunderland in the North-East of England during the 1990's, much criticized at the time because of strange manifestations, but where men of God once at loggerheads with each other were seen to embrace in repentance and mutual forgiveness. Now, I was hearing about Arab and Jew being reconciled, and I wanted to see that—and report on it—more than any other phenomenon. This was surely the greatest untold story of all, and I wanted to play my part in telling the world that the Prince of Peace has the answer to all the problems of the Middle East—and indeed of the world itself.

So when I heard that CMJ was soon holding its national UK conference in Swanwick, Derbyshire, I was keen to be part of it, the cost being met by Linda as a 64th birthday present. Naturally I wanted her to join me, so I paid for her ticket! It was a steaming hot July day, almost exactly eight years since a devastating event struck my family (and the nation) in 2005 when my younger brother David was severely injured in the 7/7 bombings of the London transport system during the morning rush hour which left 52 dead and hundreds wounded. He lost his left leg and spleen, and was battered and bruised in many places. But he made an incredibly brave recovery, thanks no doubt to prayers around the world as well as the skill of the doctors and nurses at St Mary's, Paddington. The Islamic fundamentalists failed to break his indomitable spirit as he cheerily continued his life at work as a management accountant for the Evening Standard, on the stage in amateur dramatics, as chief server at church, and even, occasionally, on the golf course or at wheelchair tennis. He and his wife Angela already had Matthew and then along came Alice Mary Jane, her last given name in honor of one of the paramedics who saved David's life.

Dates and anniversaries always mean a lot to me. So I suppose it was appropriate that this anniversary date marked the beginning of the work I was about to undertake that could help in healing the rifts, divisions, and misunderstandings that had allowed the thought of such atrocities to poison the minds of many, bringing yet further misery to our hurting and sinful world.

Shortly before Swanwick, Martin Hall, a friend from my home town of Doncaster who was already a committed supporter of Israel-oriented mission, came round for a chat. He said that he and his wife, Margaret, had been praying about future support, and felt led to offer me the opportunity of visiting Israel, possibly as part of a tour or conference, to help me learn more about what was obviously becoming a new and important ministry for me. They were prepared to pay for my flight, which they saw as an investment towards extending the Kingdom of God, especially among the Jewish people. My excitement and anticipation went up a notch as a result, and I couldn't wait for the next installment of what God had in store for me.

So when an appeal was made during the Swanwick conference for a volunteer coordinator to help prepare for the next *At the Crossroads* the following May, I once more felt that strange warmth pulsate through my spiritual antennae. They also wanted a new editor for their quarterly Prayer Focus to inform supporters of the prayer needs of their various workers around the world, and I suppose that was a "no-brainer" in view of my qualifications. But Linda couldn't at first understand why I had offered to help with the Jerusalem conference since it was about organizing rather than writing or editing.

My offer of taking over the editorship of the Prayer Focus was duly accepted, but it was three months before my offer to help with the *Crossroads* conference was accepted, by which time—by mutual consent through phone-link discussions with some of the leaders in Israel—my job description had been significantly tweaked to fit my skills and calling to their needs. My focus was to be generally on communications, while also helping to write fundraising appeals. Then during and after the event, I was to give journalistic coverage of it with the intention of raising the profile of what God was doing in the region at a time when the media focused almost exclusively on conflict.

Now my heart was racing. I was certainly up for this! What a privilege and what a challenge!

2

A Foretaste of Heaven!

When I was taken on as the Prayer Focus editor, it was emphasized that a visit to Israel would greatly help my understanding of the role. Thanks to the generous offer of my friends, Martin and Margaret Hall, this was now clearly on the cards. In the ensuing three months, by the time my conference coordinator offer had morphed into conference correspondent, an Israel visit became urgent.

CMJ Israel director Don Stanley, a lovely Australian, wanted me to come out more or less straight away—to meet staff, get a feel of the land, see the sights, and talk through my role with conference organizers—before returning in the spring for the event itself. In 64 years I had never been to Israel; now I was being asked to visit twice in six months! All the "buses" were coming at once. I was on the ceiling with excitement, mixed with a little panic at what it would all entail. It took me quite a while to come down to earth.

I was about to go, as someone quipped, "where it is all happening, where it all has happened, and where it all will happen." My first-ever visit to Israel was a greater blessing than I could ever have imagined—even "a foretaste of heaven," as one of the clergy said during the Sunday service at Christ Church in Jerusalem, the CMJ Israel headquarters which includes an extensive guest house, coffee shop, bookshop, heritage center, and much more. Built in 1849 as the first Protestant church in the Middle East, it's a beautifully tranquil oasis secure in its own compound (complete with gardens and courtyards) just inside the Old City walls of this ancient city referred to by the psalmist some 3,000 years ago as "the joy of the whole earth" (Psalm 48:2). And indeed it lives up to that with its glorious white stone reflecting the warm late autumn sunshine, its lofty position on Mount Zion and other familiar sites from the Bible and the magnificent colors of bougainvillea and other flora even at this late hour of the year set against rows of majestic palms.

The clergyman's "heaven" comment was specifically referring to the multi-national congregation that morning when large groups from Uganda and Singapore joined worshippers from many other nations in a time of powerful praise. All who took part in leading the service, including the Archbishop of Uganda, were so articulate, eloquent, and passionate, and the beautiful Kenyan liturgy added something special. The stunning building, totally restored for the bi-centenary year of 2009, was packed to the rafters amidst a heavenly atmosphere and truly wonderful worship accompanied by trumpet, grand piano, and guitar.

My trip coincided with the Jewish festival of Hanukkah (celebrating God's miraculous provision of light at yet another dark time in their history), so it was a joy to watch the lighting of the nine-branched menorah amidst a carnival atmosphere pervading the city. It was apparently the first time in 175 years that it coincided with Thanksgiving, which meant a lot to the many Americans whose company I enjoyed while there—and I did sample some pumpkin pie in Galilee!

As Jesus is "the Light of the world," * the festival's prox-
imity to Christmas is entirely apt. Hanukkah is an eight-day
festival marking God's intervention during the reign of the
ruthless Syrian-Greek emperor Antiochus Epiphanes who
desecrated the Jewish Temple by sacrificing a pig there and
blasphemously proclaimed himself God. Judah Maccabee
led a brave and successful revolt against the tyrant in 139
BC and re-established temple worship (Hanukkah means
"dedication") with the aid of the menorah which burned
miraculously for eight days despite having only enough oil
for a day. The Greeks had polluted the rest.

I loved going for walks through the ancient, winding
alleys of the Old City, trying not to linger too long through the
shuqs (market routes) as most salesmen are very persistent,
and won't take "no" for an answer, but it was all so fasci-
nating. As I traipsed along the Via Dolorosa along which,
according to tradition, Jesus carried his cross to Golgotha, it
was awesome to think my Lord had tramped these paths for
me—and you! I was particularly intrigued by the tiny doors
to many of the apartments off these ornate stone streets,
and only learned much later that they are known as the "eye
of the needle," a phrase used by Jesus to explain that it is
easier for a camel to go through the eye of a needle than for
a rich man to enter the Kingdom of God. However, nothing
is impossible with God.

But I hadn't come only as a tourist. I also had my work
cut out in terms of meeting up with key staff at their various
centers across the country and, in some cases, getting my
"marching orders" for ongoing work connected with the
conference in Jerusalem the following May. The work/life

---

* John 8:12

balance proved a tricky juggling act, made more challenging by the fact that I was having to get used to mobile phones (not one, but two) for the first time in my life, having studiously avoided them until now in a bid to protect my space and sanity.

When Linda, my wife, realized I was going to Israel she insisted that one investment of paramount importance would have to be a mobile—chiefly so we could keep in touch via texting. I am now in possession of a Smartphone, which can "sing and dance" though I have yet to discover all its many talents; just happy to have been in touch with my beloved through simple messages. My new boss, Don Stanley, also loaned me a spare mobile for making local calls and arranging meetings, and on duly discovering my technological ineptitude, teasingly branded me as "low-tech," though hopefully useful in other ways.

Martin and Margaret Hall turned out to be my guides as well as sponsors. Veteran visitors to Israel, they had also booked a flight for themselves for a trip without an itinerary. They knew they should go, but had no specific reason for doing so—until they discovered CMJ had asked if I could come out at the same time! It's wonderful how God prepares the way. They were renting an apartment on the Hebron Road from a Messianic Jewish speaker they supported. They showed me around many of the amazing sights, though I am also indebted to two other experts in this field for their inspiring guidance: Ariel Keren-Or, a Jewish Brazilian international speaker, and Netanel, a Jewish New Zealander.

Despite hardly a wink of sleep on the flight, I continued sampling the sights, sounds, and smells of Jerusalem. Wide-eyed, I beheld the magnificent vistas before me: looking over a deep valley towards the Mount of Olives, standing on the very stones where Jesus stood trial (all excavated in recent years), and being shown around the apparently genuine location of the Upper Room, still to be formally announced by the Israeli Department of Antiquities. I touched the Western Wall (the remains of the Temple destroyed by the Romans which makes it particularly holy to Jews), tasted delicious meals at Arab and Jewish-run restaurants and bars (as well as in the Christ Church center itself), and made some deep friendships.

Getting to know the people I would be working with and their organization was, of course, the highlight of my trip. However, before I introduce all of the new (and old) friends I made, let me tell you about the extraordinary organization to which I now belonged.

3

An Amazing Ministry

Working behind the scenes in putting together the *At the Crossroads* conference is a 200-year-old Anglican organization known as the *Church's Ministry Among Jewish People* (CMJ) whose influence and accomplishments are very impressive, as I learned from Robin Aldridge, former CMJ-UK director, during an in-depth interview back in 2009.

There have been times in the past when mission organizations influenced the ruling authorities of nations. David Livingstone, for example, became an adviser to the British Government and has since been remembered possibly more as an explorer than a missionary, which is unfair because his primary aim in Africa was always to preach Christ. In today's Britain, few are aware of the part played by CMJ in one of the most significant political changes of the modern world.

Conceived in 1809, CMJ is a Church of England society, whose founding fathers included such luminaries as William Wilberforce and the Earl of Shaftesbury. The organization has steadfastly worked among Jewish communities around the world, and has been instrumental in fulfilling many ancient Biblical prophecies. Chief among these is the restoration of Jews to the Holy Land from all corners of the globe, a phenomenon foretold by Isaiah, Jeremiah, Ezekiel, and others.

Such a scenario, the prophets indicated, would be regarded as a greater miracle even than the crossing of the Red Sea in their escape from slavery in Egypt as God's chosen people would return to their roots from the north, south, east, and west. After nearly 2,000 years of dispersal in countries far and wide, Israel would be reborn and once more take its place among the nations.

It was politicians (and preachers) like Wilberforce, responsible for the abolition of slavery in the UK, whose far-sighted understanding of the Scriptures helped to found CMJ. The French Revolution left the British aristocracy nervous (in view of royalty axed at the guillotine), while the middle classes generally recognized that the dark days in which they were living matched some of the signs Jesus said would precede His coming again. But they also understood that the Master would not return before His people, the Jews, were a) back in the land and b) worshipping Him as Messiah.

Jeremiah, for example, speaks both of their return to the land and to the Lord, "'See, I will bring them from the land of the north and gather them from the ends of the earth'" shortly followed by "'This is the covenant that I will make with the house of Israel after that time,' declares the Lord. 'I will put my law in their minds and write it on their hearts. I will be their God, and they will be my people'" (31:8, 33).

So, in view of the fact that many Jews had already taken refuge on their own doorstep in the East End of London, fleeing persecution in Europe, the CMJ founders decided to make a start on reaching them with the message of Yeshua (Jesus) as their Messiah.

It's not as though Jews had never been part of the Church, of course, as the first-century "Christians" were almost entirely Jewish. But tragically, as Gentiles came to predominate, they cut themselves off from their Hebraic roots and some even came to believe they had replaced Israel in God's affections, a diabolical "theology" which in turn planted the seeds of the Holocaust as anti-Semitism spread like gangrene. But thanks to the Puritans and subsequent evangelical revivals under Wesley and others, a Biblical understanding of God's plan for the Jews was recovered.

The so-called Messianic Jewish movement itself has just marked its bicentenary, having effectively begun in London's East End with the formation of Benei Abraham (Children of Abraham), on September 9, 1813, as a result of the work of CMJ. Jewish believers in Jesus as Messiah encountered difficulties that Gentiles did not, such as rejection by their families and community, and even loss of employment. So this was a forum enabling them to relate to each other in a Jewish cultural setting. And an initial "trickle" of 41 members has since turned into a torrent encompassing hundreds of thousands that, in fulfillment of the Scriptures, will eventually become a mighty river.

The level of interest in the work of CMJ—of taking the message of Jesus "to the Jew first" (Romans 1:16)—was such that earlier that year (on April 7, 1813), 20,000 people watched the laying of the foundation stone by the Duke of Kent (father of Queen Victoria) for a large complex in Bethnal Green known as Palestine Place, which was to comprise a chapel (where Benei Abraham held their meetings), a school, housing, and more.

CMJ established centers all over Europe and the Mediterranean, and in the 1840s built a church in Jerusalem—the only Protestant church in what was then the Ottoman Empire—which doubled as a consulate for the British Government. It was on the basis of the consul needing a "chapel" that permission was eventually granted to build Christ Church, which is still an important focus for the society's activities.

Through influence in high places, which had marked its progress from the beginning, CMJ came into its own when, almost a century ago, the Balfour Declaration of 1917 spelled out the British government's promise to provide a home in "Palestine"—still then under Turkish control—for the Jewish people. Within weeks General Allenby's forces liberated Jerusalem, and the way was open to fulfill the promised declaration.

More than partly mindful of Arab opposition to these plans, however, Britain wavered on their obligations and forcefully prevented Jews returning to the Holy Land. It wasn't until 1948, after another war and the murder of millions of God's chosen people—many of whom could otherwise have escaped to safety—that finally even the United Nations recognized the new state.

Meanwhile, as CMJ focused on reaching Jewish communities all over Europe and North Africa with the Gospel, specifically through establishing schools, significant progress was made. It is estimated that by the time of the outbreak of World War II in 1939, there were as many as 100,000 Jews who believed Jesus was their Messiah.

The excellence of their education is well demonstrated by the fact that one man living in Morocco sent his child to the CMJ School in Cairo, a thousand miles away!

There were large Jewish communities in Europe—some 500,000 in Warsaw alone, most of whom were wiped out by the Nazis, and about a million in Hungary. But they had also settled in Cairo, Tunisia, Ethiopia, and Morocco. For example, in 1939, Jews represented a quarter of the population of Casablanca, making it the "New York" of North Africa. Growing Islamization, however, caused many to emigrate to Israel, where the believers among them helped to form the embryo of the Messianic movement there, while many of the European believers were victims of the Holocaust.

Among CMJ's key areas of operation were the Falasha Jews of Ethiopia, many of whom came to recognize Jesus as Messiah and later took part in Operation Moses—the secret airlifting to the Promised Land. This too helped to boost the then fledgling Messianic movement which has now become a significant worldwide phenomenon with thriving fellowships (many a mix of Jew and Arab) scattered all over Israel.

Among those who have facilitated the work of CMJ over the years was Russian aristocrat Baron von Ustinov (grandfather of British actor Peter Ustinov) along with various kings and kaisers. In fact, Germany was particularly helpful over the years, all the more ironic in view of the Jews' fate at the hands of the Nazis.

In Rumania, a young Jew called Richard Wurmbrand turned from communism to Christ through the efforts of CMJ and became their foremost evangelist who subsequently suffered extensively, spending many years in prison being tortured for his beliefs.

Speaking at Auschwitz in 2010 at the 65th anniversary of its liberation, Binyamin Netanyahu said he saw the modern Jewish state emerging from the Holocaust as a fulfillment of

Ezekiel's prophecy of dry bones coming back to life.[1] Nearly a century earlier, CMJ made exactly the same comparison in a May 1918 publication that followed the collapse of the Turkish Empire.[2] And at CMJ's Annual General Meeting the following year, the Bishop of Armagh said, "No reader of prophecy, I think, can fail to see that God is working out in our time the fulfillment of the latter-day promises regarding the Jew ... I believe that ... we are preparing for the great future that God has for the Jews...."[3]

And when Britain was then officially offered the mandate over Palestine, it was fully endorsed by CMJ who said:

> "As citizens of the Empire we are ... thankful beyond measure that, in the Providence of God, our nation has been chosen for preparing the Holy Land for the great future that lies before it.... We regard the incorporation of the Balfour Declaration of 1917 in the Peace Treaty with Turkey ... as one of the most wonderful instances on record of the working out of God's promises to the nation he loves with an everlasting love.
>
> "Why is it that the Christian public today is so deeply interested [sadly, hardly the case in 2014] in the coming return of the Jews to the Holy Land? Because students of Holy Writ know... that a time is coming when 'all Israel shall be saved,' and when the Jews will rejoice in their Messiah, and that previous to the turning of the nation to Christ must first come the re-establishment of the Chosen Race in their own land....

---

1 Netanyahu Auschwitz Speech Parts 1 and 2, YouTube, https://www.youtube.com/watch?v=BAuZA17genk

2 Kelvin Crombie, *Restoring Israel: 200 Years of the CMJ Story,* 2008, p. 133.

3 Crombie, ibid, p. 134.

> "It is our duty as a society to send missionaries in and out amongst the Jews, bringing the remnant according to grace into the fellowship of the Gospel, and preparing the nation as a whole for that great day when the Jews shall 'look on him whom they pierced' and acknowledge him as their Messiah" (Zechariah 12:10).[4]

CMJ endured much opposition over the years, especially from Jewish rabbis. In one extraordinary episode in the 1860s a group of missionaries in Abyssinia (now Ethiopia) had to be freed from four years of captivity by the British Army after the Emperor was apparently snubbed by Queen Victoria over a request to send an ambassador to England. Even the Archbishop of Canterbury had called Britain to prayer for the release of the prisoners.

One of those imprisoned in the cliff-top fortress, known as Magdala, was a man named Moritz Hall, whose Ethiopian wife gave birth to a daughter on the day Magdala was stormed by General Napier's troops. The baby was named Magdalena, and was destined to be the future wife of Baron von Ustinov (who subsequently settled in Jaffa, Israel, where he facilitated CMJ work) and grandmother of Peter Ustinov, the famous British actor. In fact, the Baron's palatial property is now a CMJ center and guest home known as Beit Immanuel.

There will be more battles to come, no doubt, but CMJ will have fulfilled its task when the Jews, already now back in their ancient homeland, take a big step further by demonstrating national recognition for their Messiah.

---

4 Crombie, ibid, p. 134.

Note: Read more CMJ history at their various country websites. See bibliography for the web addresses.

4

Getting Acquainted

Meeting the CMJ Board Members

A week into my stay in Israel, I left Jerusalem to spend a day with some of the CMJ Board members. We met at the CMJ's Beit Immanuel center in Jaffa, just south of Tel Aviv. It's a very special place. Hosting a guest house as well as two thriving congregations, the 1869 building, originally known as the "palace" of the aforementioned Russian aristocrat Baron von Ustinov, is badly in need of refurbishing at a cost of $7 million. And plans to restore it to its former glory (and more) are well underway. Fundraising possibilities was the subject of our meeting, which concluded with a wonderful meal at a nearby Italian restaurant where it was great to renew fellowship with Pedro Santos, the Beit Immanuel director, whom I had met during his recent tour of the UK.

(I have since more or less managed to replicate the spinach pasta I chose and have served it to Linda—and others—several times. It was absolutely delicious—with mushrooms, red peppers, thinly-sliced sweet potatoes, red onions, herbs, and olive oil.)

I learned much on the trip back to Jerusalem in the CMJ people-carrier, expertly driven by Christ Church center manager, Linda Cohen, who weaved her way through the crazy traffic with all the juggling skills she clearly uses in running the complex itself. We were accompanied by the Dean of St.

Andrew's Cathedral in Singapore, the Very Reverend Kuan Kim Seng, whose church caters to thousands of worshippers and who runs seventeen services each weekend. (The title "Very" is attributed to deans.) **Rev. Sharon Hayton,**[1] the Canadian director, shared about the Holy Spirit outpouring among the Inuits of the Arctic Circle. Much feverish conversation ensued during which even a book I was reading, *A Durable Peace* by Binyamin Netanyahu (loaned by the CMJ Israel Director, my new boss), added further fuel to my growing conviction of the connection between the rise of Zionism (promoting the return of the Jews to the Holy Land) and the outpouring of the Holy Spirit among the Gentiles. The rise of Zionism through Theodore Herzl (and others) began in earnest in 1897 just at the time the modern Pentecostal movement was about to be birthed. The year 1967, when the Jews regained control of their capital Jerusalem for the first time in more than 2,000 years, was also highly significant in that it coincided with the outpouring of the Holy Spirit among many of the old established churches (known as the Charismatic Movement). Conversely, the denial of such movements as being of the Holy Spirit has, I believe, contributed to the Holocaust, and currently contributes to some of the anti-Semitism and "replacement theology" (that the church has replaced Israel in God's purposes). There's much more to this, and I have expanded on it somewhat in a later chapter. Jaffa, by the way, is the ancient port of Joppa, where St. Peter had the vision that persuaded him the Gospel was for Gentiles too!

---

1 The many names of my new and old friends are mentioned for the sake of those readers who might know them. The names that are significant to the rest of the book, or that are mentioned more than once in this chapter, are rendered in bold in this chapter.

Spiritual Attack

Both Linda (very busy at home with Christmas projects in primary schools) and I came under attack on the health front at various times during the fortnight. I also lost quite a bit of sleep thanks to diving mosquitoes. On one occasion I had just boarded what we would call a Supertram (an excellent new form of transport in Jerusalem known there as the Light Railway) when I received an urgent text from Linda, "Please pray, I'm losing my voice...." I was due to meet **Martin and Margaret Hall**, along with Keren Pryor (widow of well-known Hebraic roots teacher, Dwight), in Zion Square. But Board members **Martin Weatherston, Rev. Sharon Hayton**, and **Dr. Theresa Newell** (who wrote the foreword to this book) had in the meantime also bumped into them, and so when I alighted from my stop I requested that we all gather round in a circle to pray for Linda, who subsequently recovered—praise the Lord! It was a special treat to have been able to get to know Keren, who is originally from Durban (my neck of the woods) though more latterly from Dayton, Ohio, and her young friend Caitlin, also from Dayton.

I should mention that buying a ticket for the tram proved quite a challenge to my "low-tech" brain. Though there was an English option among the many buttons on the platform machine, the instructions seemed to keep reverting to Hebrew and I missed the first train as I was left bamboozled and panicking. Thankfully, a young Jewish man came to the rescue, as they often did when they saw foreigners struggling. I am, however, proud to say that on at least two occasions I was delighted to be able to give directions to others wanting to know their way around!

0004200719

Sell your books at sellbackyourBook.com!

Go to sellbackyourBook.com
and get an instant price
quote. We even pay the
shipping - see what your old
books are worth today!

Holocaust Wake-Up Call

The reason for the tram ride was that I had joined a party of Ugandans that morning for a visit to the Holocaust Museum (Yad Vashem) on the outskirts of the city. **David Pileggi**, rector of Christ Church and *At the Crossroads* spokesman, led us on a three-and-a-half hour tour which left no stone unturned in portraying the sheer horror of the rise of Nazism, and how their evil, pagan policies led to the extermination of six million Jews while many, including much of the church, looked the other way.

It's a wake-up call, especially in view of Iran's oft-repeated threat to wipe Israel off the map. But the West is going soft on the issue, as they gullibly believe the country's nuclear development is for peaceful purposes—shades of 1938 and Neville Chamberlain talking of "peace in our time." David was so gentle and loving with our African brethren, which included the Archbishop of Uganda and other bishops. "Come this way, Uganda," he would call out as he prepared to explain another exhibition, addressing them always as "My dear friends."

Later, while discussing my role in the Christ Church courtyard with **David Pileggi** and Michael Kerem (an extraordinary guy who has travelled much in the Middle East and on whose vision the Crossroads conference is based), David kept rebuking Eleanor, the cat, for persecuting the lizards of the garden, which was plainly unnecessary, as she was so well fed already. And the midday prayers at the neighboring mosque, turned up to full volume, rudely drowned out our conversation. David threatened to complain, though I think he was joking!

My remit was simply to produce "good copy" on the conference itself as well as pre-conference fundraising appeals, which I think I managed with the help of some powerful testimonies (included in this book). I was told that £30,000 (about $45,000) was the target to meet expenses, the main cost being the transportation of Muslim-background believers who could not afford the trip. And it worked out at £250 ($375) for each of 120 invited participants, significantly the same number who met in the Upper Room on the Day of Pentecost and turned the world upside down, which proved a good line. As I put it, "Perhaps you, or your church, can sponsor a delegate and so partner in a very practical way towards the fulfillment of prophecy, the Great Commission, and genuine reconciliation only possible through the Prince of Peace?" It worked well with congregations I know, who responded very generously.

I should also mention the Wednesday night Bible studies, run by **David Pileggi** (with **Don Stanley**, CMJ Israel director, my new boss, standing in the first week), during which we looked at chapters 16 & 17 of the Book of Revelation. And it *was* a "revelation" as they were the best I've ever attended, commendably well led while also encouraging much participation in a bid to find answers to some deep issues. What struck me most was the fact that we were discussing earth-shaking events predicted in the Bible for the days immediately preceding the Second Coming in the very city where much of it is scheduled to take place.

Out into the Wilderness

My friends and "guides," **Martin and Margaret,** hired a car for a week, so we initially took an afternoon trip down to Qumran, where the ancient Dead Sea scrolls were discovered in 1947. While waiting on a stone wall in Prophets Street (Hanavi'im) to be picked up, I had an amazing experience reading the Scriptures (appropriately from the prophet Isaiah chapters 51-54) which talk so much of Jerusalem, and it all came so alive with new revelation. It was as if the very stones on which I was sitting were crying out, "Behold your God, who walked these streets, and who died here, just a few hundred yards away, for the sins of the whole world!"

The temperature in Qumran rose to 29 °C, but it was very dry and most pleasant. I was amazed by the scenery of the Judean wilderness as we descended to the depths of 1,200 ft. below sea level, the lowest point on earth. Such extraordinarily rough and barren terrain, dotted with the occasional Bedouin settlement, brought home to me how treacherous it must have been for the Good Samaritan going down the road to Jericho, and indeed how amazing a ministry Jesus had in drawing people from all over such apparently impassable territory to hear him.

Next day we drove up the Jordan Valley to Galilee, where "the people walking in darkness have seen a great light" (Isaiah 9:2), but not before we were stopped at a checkpoint and asked to produce our passports. I had left mine behind at Christ Church, but (no doubt partly thanks to silent prayers to be spared the embarrassment of arrest) my driving license sufficed. We stayed at Beit Bracha, the CMJ guest house at Migdal (the home village of Mary Magdalene), although it was actually full so we were accommodated next door at Beit Shalom, commanding breathtaking views of the Sea of Galilee and the Golan Heights on the other side. There were lots of South Africans there, along with Mauritians, and we shared a Shabbat dinner hosted by Linda Walker, who runs the center with her husband Ted, who was away at a retreat. We spent a bit of time in Tiberias, just a few miles south and the main resort on the shores of Galilee where friends Alan and Daphne Brooke stayed with their family for several years in the early 1980s as Alan, a dentist, had offered his services in a bid to help rebuild the Jewish state. As we enjoyed refreshments on the veranda of a restaurant in Tiberias on the second evening, it could have been sub-tropical Durban in midsummer—it was November 30.

Also at Migdal, we visited the first century boat (of the kind Jesus and his disciples may well have used) recently discovered embedded in the mud there. And then we motored a few miles further north to the ruins of Capernaum and were reminded of Jesus' rebuke that, in not recognizing their Messiah, they would "go down to the depths (hades)" (Luke 10:15). Another prophecy fulfilled before our eyes! We travelled across country (racing past Cana and Nazareth) to Mount Carmel, near Haifa on the Mediterranean coast, just in time for a Shabbat (Saturday) service at the Carmel Assembly led by **David and Karen Davis**, originally from New York's Times Square Church founded by David Wilkerson of *The Cross and the Switchblade* fame. They were first called to Israel specifically to work among drug addicts after hearing about the problem from an Arab family they befriended in

Jerusalem's Old City. Sent out by Wilkerson's church, they have been at Mt. Carmel many years and have established a thriving congregation of both Arabs and Jews while at the same time helping to feed and clothe the poor and running a drug rehabilitation center.

Karen led a very joyful time of worship and Peter Tsukahira (a Japanese-American) gave an inspiring sermon on having your eyes on the Lord when no one else can help you (2 Chronicles 20). The service was conducted in four languages, with Hebrew translated into English, or the other way around, from the front (by an Arab), and headsets available in both Arabic and Russian as there are many Russian Jewish immigrants in Israel who have yet to learn Hebrew. We afterwards enjoyed a delicious meal at a café run by a member of the congregation and bought some exquisite works of art from her father, a Romanian Jew my age. We then stopped at Mount Carmel itself, where Elijah faced down the false prophets of Baal in a great contest of deciding who was God! The view over the Jezreel Valley (the Plain of Armageddon) was very dramatic, and there is a statue of the great prophet along with an altar, chapel, and garden—all part of a Carmelite Monastery.

Nearby Cana has particular resonance for me as it was there—where Jesus performed his first miracle, of turning water into wine at a wedding—that my wife Linda (in the year 2000) had a vision of her own wedding before meeting me six months later! See my earlier book, *Israel the Chosen*, for more details.

Other Extraordinary Connections

Chief among my new deep friendships was with **Martin Weatherston**, CMJ's Australia director and vice-chairman of the International Board, which was holding its annual meetings while I was there. The two of us were invited to what turned out to be a wonderful Shabbat (Sabbath) dinner on my first Friday night by **Don Stanley** and his wife, **Caroline**, so we walked together up the empty streets of Jerusalem (even secular Jews still take the Sabbath very seriously) discovering more about each other along the way. Naturally we had initially assumed we were part of an *Ashes* encounter between a genuine Oz from Perth, Western Australia, and a tried and trusted Pom from the North of England. But it gradually dawned on us that our paths had crossed many times in the past. Not only were we both South Africans, but we even went to the same boarding school—and at the same time! We don't remember each other from then as we were in different houses, but we would no doubt have passed each other many times on the way to and from classes, sports fields, and halls of residence.

There were other connections, too. **Martin** was later assistant to Bill Burnett, then Archbishop of Cape Town, who had earlier experienced an extraordinary encounter with the Holy Spirit as he prayed in Grahamstown Cathedral, where he was previously bishop. Bill had encouraged me early in my Christian life with personal letters, as he had also been our parish priest and family friend during my childhood years in Ladysmith, KwaZulu-Natal. In this role, Martin was also linked with Cecil Kerr, visionary behind the Christian Renewal Center in Northern Ireland, working and praying for reconciliation across the Catholic and Protestant divide. My Linda was part of that community for several years! And the paths crossed again when Martin's wife Kim texted him to say she had just renewed a Facebook connection with Trish, wife of my best friend from schooldays, Julian Southey. We still keep in touch with them!

As I told Linda at the time, my head was in an absolute spin with the myriads of people I kept meeting and then having deep conversations with as if I'd known them all my life. My friendship with **Martin** in particular seemed to blossom by the minute—we even shared a bottle of Cape Red wine on the balcony of my room one evening. It did become a bit confusing, though, regularly meeting up with two Martins—this new good friend, **Martin Weatherston**, and my sponsor and guide, **Martin Hall**.

Martin W was very encouraging about my role at the forthcoming conference in getting news out of the reconciliation already taking place in the Middle East to a public largely kept in the dark by a skeptical media and, in many cases, by churches that have drifted from their Hebraic roots, if not cut themselves off altogether. He explained that CMJ walked something of a tightrope in this area, ever-conscious of the need to balance their calling of making Messiah Jesus known to the Jews with sensitivity to the authorities and ultra-Orthodox groups who see this as an intrusion. So clearly I would be walking a tightrope in my attempts to let the world know that God is at work in Jerusalem. No pressure then! But a privilege nonetheless. After all, "How beautiful on the mountains are the feet of those who bring good news… who proclaim salvation, who say to Zion, 'Your God reigns!'" (Isaiah 52:7).

Rev. John Atkinson, the CMJ South African director and chairman of the Board, arrived later and it turned out that he had recently presided over the funeral of my beloved god-mother Elizabeth Topping, a committed member of Christ Church, Kenilworth, in Cape Town who had also witnessed my birth in that city back in 1949. He had even escorted two of her daughters on a trip to Israel!

Another extraordinary link involved Chris and Colleen Courtois, from KwaZulu-Natal, working as volunteers at Christ Church. When I told them I came from Ladysmith, Colleen turned to her husband asking, "I wonder what happened to Ailsa?" I was happy to be able to tell them that she now lives in Cambridge, New Zealand. Ailsa Henderson is a very close family friend, so much so that she virtually became a daughter to my father during his latter days with his own children scattered abroad. In fact, the book I wrote about Dad, *Doctor on the Run*, was dedicated to her! Colleen had taught with her at Pietermaritzburg Technical College. And Chris, a veteran of the famous 56-mile Comrades Marathon which my father ran 29 times, asked Colleen to add the book to his Christmas list. With all the teeming millions surrounding us every day, it's still such a small world!

Also among the volunteers was an Indian-South African from Port Shepstone—I had many childhood holidays at nearby beaches. Shanda was very sweet and helpful, and I had the pleasure of getting to know Deepak Kataria, a convert from Hinduism who is from Bangalore in India but working as a missionary in the Philippines.

There was also a double link with my early Christian life in England. **Dr. Theresa Newell**, from Pittsburgh, USA, was another Board member with whom I had many wonderful conversations. We shared a love for Rev. John Stott, who had a major influence on my life while I worshipped at All Souls in London during the 1970s. It was through his preaching that I felt called to journalism. Theresa, who was herself a journalist on the Birmingham News (Alabama) during the civil rights marches when she was at times threatened by white supremacists, actually knew John better than I did as she frequently had him to stay—he had even been involved in setting up the seminary she and her husband Bruce (now a retired admiral) had started. We talked of how John had a bit of a "blind spot" over the Jewish issue and how she had once rebuked him after he had expounded Romans chapter 1 line by line in his usual meticulous way but had stopped short of explaining (or even mentioning) the phrase that the Gospel was "to the Jew first." However, we both agreed that he was an extremely humble man who had a towering influence on Christendom. Theresa was always great to have around—never short of having something edifying or funny (or both) to say. I would describe her as 72 going on 27! We have since continued our friendship by email and recently collaborated on writing a feature about Martin Luther King to coincide with the new film Selma, focusing on the civil rights movement. Theresa has been a huge encouragement to me since I've taken on this role.

The other link, in this regard, was with Jean Herrick, with whom I was reunited at the UK conference at Swanwick—40 years after I had corresponded with her as one of the tasks assigned to me during my early days at All Souls when she had been working for CMJ among the Falasha Jews of Ethiopia. Jean subsequently handed over the role of editing the organization's quarterly Prayer Focus to me and effectively became my mentor.

I had a good long chat one evening with Shirley, a volunteer from Preston, Lancashire (though originally from Glasgow), who actually knew Helen MacIntosh, the Jewish lady who led the "nursery class" for new Christians at All Souls and became a virtual "spiritual mother" to me.

I also met the charming Jane Stewart, a Board member from Ireland, Bishop Michael Obasuyi and his lovely wife, Pat, from London, and found myself in the reception room one day summarizing the history of CMJ to Richard, a visiting vicar from Wimbledon, London, who was calling in on behalf of an elderly parishioner who was actually married at Christ Church.

And I had a chat with Yoel Seton, director of Shoresh Tours—also based at Christ Church—which conducts tours aimed at connecting Christians with their Hebraic roots (Shoresh is Hebrew for *roots*). Sharing with me the importance of their tourists encountering God, Yoel was quite frank, saying, "Unless God touches people while they're on tour, there's no point in being in the business."

And it clearly does happen because my wife Linda's first visit to Israel 20 years earlier was with a Shoresh Tour which included a stay at Christ Church and obviously made a big impression on her.

Going to School

I may be low-tech, but I *can* read maps (forget GPS) and with the aid of the excellent maps given out by the Tourist Information office, I managed to find my way around the parts of Jerusalem I needed to locate for the purpose of meeting key CMJ workers with whom I would be corresponding at regular intervals as editor of the Prayer Focus.

At the Anglican International School, situated appropriately on Hanavi'im (Prophets) Street, I had a fruitful meeting with outgoing head Owen Hoskin, from New Zealand, and his successor Lawrence Hilditch, from Northern Ireland, who are clearly both doing a great job as they passionately oversee fine teaching establishments while also engaging in leadership at Christ Church itself. Next door is the Makor HaTikvah, a school run specifically on Messianic Jewish lines and led by Cookie Schwaeber-Issan who I missed because they were closed for Hanukkah but with whom I had a brief telephone conversation. I also got to know Joy Marshall (Don Stanley's PA) and Erik Rogers, the Anglican school's business resources manager from Atlanta, Georgia. And I successfully located Remi Rauh, whom we knew from Ireland days. He now runs an Arabic Christian bookstore and, though I met Remi's lovely wife Laura, I missed Remi himself and their two children each time I called.

Bookstore and Garden Tomb

I made several visits to the Immanuel Bookshop at Christ Church, introducing myself to Marilyn Jelski, an Argentinian Jewess who made Aliyah (the term for "coming home" to the Promised Land) and is now in charge of the shop, which was always a hive of activity and where I had "extra business" as my own book is now available there. An estate agent friend of Marilyn's, a Sephardic Jew from Spain, tried to encourage me to make Aliyah on the basis that space for the Sephardim has been especially reserved in the Negev (desert) in the south of the country! I'm not sure I qualify, as it was my great-grandfather who, as a Sephardic Jew from Portugal, was hounded out of the country and left for the Americas, but she assured me that I did. I also had a delightful chat in the bookshop with an Afrikaner lady who had five children now living on four continents, including a daughter in Israel.

I found my visit to the Garden Tomb an especially moving experience—no one is quite sure whether this (or the Church of the Holy Sepulchre nearby) is the genuine site of Jesus' crucifixion, burial, and resurrection, but the rough shape of a skull cut out of the rock on the side of an adjacent hill (now incongruously overlooking a noisy Arab bus station) is quite convincing. Jesus was executed by the roadside at Golgotha (meaning "the place of the skull") outside the city wall. I couldn't get a picture of the "empty tomb" entrance because of the crowds waiting to catch a glimpse inside. But the beautiful hymn-singing of a tour group from Jamaica (where my half-Jewish grandmother came from) lifted the soul as it wafted through the gracious garden tended with loving care by the British-based Garden Tomb Association whose volunteers are clearly committed to keeping faith with the genuine Gospel story. At last, I was proud to be British (well, I have lived there for over 40 years)!

I was blessed to have shared many meals with a delightful couple of volunteers from Pittsburgh, Pennsylvania—Dan (a former missionary pilot in Bolivia) and Neva Handley. They serve the Lord with such grace and humility, and I shared with them the story of Jane Haining, a Scottish missionary to Hungary who died in Auschwitz for the "crime" of loving the Jewish girls in her care. Her story is told by a descendant, Lynley Smith, in a book called *From Matron to Martyr* (Tate Publishing) and is available from Amazon. The couple immediately ordered the book, downloaded it onto their Kindle and had read it within days, thoroughly inspired by the courage of this marvelous woman. I had linked up with the author, who lives in New Zealand, as a result of publishing my own book and had no idea that Linda, my wife, had simultaneously discovered the story of Jane on the internet. And it was not until she was in the middle of sharing this remarkable testimony with primary pupils in school assemblies that I realized we were both digging in the same goldmine. There's obviously something special about it, and indeed the Hungarian government has recently accorded much honor to Jane. Lynley's book has now been translated into their language.

A word of advice to future tourists: Watch out for Israeli drivers who do not treat a zebra crossing as a free "get onto the road" card for pedestrians. Wait for the green light for walkers, and even then, keep your eyes on the back of your head because motorists still seem to have the right of way! And if you want a midday snack, Israelis don't know the meaning of the word "sandwich." What you're likely to get is a pile of pita bread accompanied by endless plates of a variety of salads, hummus, chillies, and relishes—probably enough to keep you going for the next 24 hours, which could be just as well, as eating out is quite expensive.

I spent my last breakfast in the delightful company of Ray Lockhart, from Bath, who was rector at Christ Church for many years and was also CMJ Israel director for a time. When I mentioned him to Linda, she remembered him from visits he made to Ireland. I still had much to do on a frantic final morning before catching my flight—and this included shopping for Arab headdresses which Linda wanted for costumes to help with presenting the Christmas message. So I was very grateful to have finally met Sue Mottershead, another Board member (from Eastbourne, Sussex), just in time for her to direct both **Martin W** and myself to the Ali Baba Souvenir Shop where it was nice to be able to browse without harassment while drinking the proprietor Shaaban's excellent tea. We were also accompanied by **Dr. Theresa Newell**, and it was such a fun shopping expedition mostly spent talking feverishly about so many important things relating to the land we had all come to love.

I haven't mentioned that the weather throughout my stay was wonderful (around 20-25°C) considering the time of year and, though I managed several runs through the streets of Jerusalem and up onto the Peace Forest promenade over-looking the Mount of Olives, I have to admit that on one occasion I did get lost, taking a wrong turn as darkness fell on my way back.

People asked me if I felt nervous in light of the security issues surrounding Israel. I have actually never been in a city that exuded such peace—especially when the streets clear on the Sabbath—though heavily armed young soldiers (boys and girls who were no more than teenagers) kept popping up all over the place. But they were hardly menacing; simply proud to defend their country against onslaughts from every side. And you felt safer for it. But there was one unnerving incident in which an Arab seemed to be making provocative gestures to a group of Jewish men in religious clothing, the latter defusing the situation by refusing to take the bait.

The Benefits of Sabbath Rest

Talking of the Sabbath, I was especially impressed by the beneficial effects of its observance. As Jesus said, "Sabbath was made for man; not man for the Sabbath," (Mark 2:27) in answer to legalistic religious critics who condemned Him for healing on a day of rest. If your donkey is in a ditch, as He put it, then get him out! If your car has broken down, call the breakdown service! Don't make a burden out of what was supposed to be a blessing. I love what author Michele Guinness says about it in her excellent book, *Woman—The Full Story: A Dynamic Celebration of Freedoms*:

> Leisure is not an optional extra. It is a spiritual requirement. Observing a Sabbath is one of the most ignored commandments in our shop-till-you-drop society—at our peril! Rest and recreation were given not just for our enjoyment, but because they are necessary to us. With its compulsory observation for a full 24 hours, from sundown to sundown, Sabbath is a useful tool against workaholism. "I have to go home now—it's my religion!" may well be worth a try. There are a disproportionate number of successful Jewish career women. They appear much less neurotic about reconciling woman as mother and worker. It could well be that Sabbath has helped them to maintain the vital balance of work and play. ... [And she quotes a Hebrew writer as saying,] "More than the Jewish people kept the Sabbath, the Sabbath kept the Jewish people."
>
> ... Some seem to think Jesus put an end to any need for a Sabbath. Far from it. He put an end to Sabbatarianism—the legalistic observation of it—but he loved the Sabbath, that weekly opportunity to climb off the merry-go-round and catch a glimpse of what eternal rest will be like. To maintain our *shalom*, a healthy integration of body, mind and spirit, we need space for reflection and recreation, time to mop the

floor and wash our smalls,[2] and a chance to be fully involved in a local faith community. All are essential if we are to maintain our God-focus.[3]

When visiting the Western Wall (the remains of Solomon's Temple and the holiest site in Judaism), I didn't think anything of it when an orthodox Jew raced past me with his hand covering his eyes as I assumed he was shielding them from the late afternoon sun. But my more knowledgeable friends pointed out that it was because I was goyim (a Gentile) and he was trying to avoid catching sight of me in such a holy place.

Ariel Keren-Or, the Brazilian Messianic Jewish international speaker who lives in Jerusalem, had also pointed out the mount on which the United Nations building now stands, apparently the very spot where the devil tempted Jesus with all the kingdoms of the world if only he would bow down and worship him! Jesus refused of course, replying that it was written: "Worship the Lord your God, and serve him only." (Matthew 4:10b) The UN is not the answer to the problems of the Middle East—Jesus is!

I have only just touched on the myriad experiences I had, concertinaed into a fortnight, which inevitably caused me at times to feel somewhat overwhelmed and under pressure. But once I resolved to seek the Lord's guidance for every step I took and every momentous encounter, I was well able to cope with the head-spinning excitement of it all.

Yet I thought perhaps I had asked too much in praying that I would have the privilege of leading a Jewish person to his/her Messiah before the trip was over. Even before we had

---

2 British for underwear
3 Michele Guinness, *Woman—The Full Story: A Dynamic Celebration of Freedoms,* Zondervan, 2003, pp. 284-285.

left London, travelling in the minibus transporting us from the car park to our terminal, I had an animated conversation touching on the spiritual reasons for going to Israel with a dentist from Portsmouth who was visiting Bangkok for the umpteenth time as he continues to introduce an innovative molding for patients. So when, for the return flight from Tel Aviv to Heathrow, I found myself sitting next to a young Jewish mum called Sophie, it didn't surprise me that we got into conversation, though she was clearly very tired, having flown out just for a day to be interviewed for a job heading up a Jewish charity helping poor Russian immigrants. She was from Hampstead (where my mum, younger brother, and his family live) and a Sephardic Jew. When she asked what I had been doing in Israel, I found myself explaining what CMJ was all about, which naturally led to an explanation of Ezekiel's prophecy of a twofold restoration—first physical, then spiritual—for the Jewish people. I trust the Lord will do the rest. And that is, after all, what CMJ (and my involvement with them) is all about!

5

Arab and Jew Embrace

The day finally arrived—May 6, 2014—for my return visit, and as the thrust of the jet engines launched our Boeing 767-300 down the Heathrow runway at full throttle, a surge of unprecedented excitement swept over me. Of course, flying was not a new experience for me. I travelled alone (under the watchful eye of an air hostess) in an old four-prop Skymaster plane from Cape Town to Port Elizabeth as a three-year-old way back in 1952. And I often accompanied my dad, who was a flying instructor in his spare time.

What made this flight so special was my destination. And not only was I flying out to Israel on that nation's 66th birthday, but I was also engaged on a mission working towards the spiritual re-birth of the Jewish people.

As a volunteer for CMJ, I was to cover this unique conference, witnessing the reconciliation of Arab and Jewish pastors who would be seeking ways of helping each other. For example, many of the delegates are from Muslim-run countries where following Jesus is a costly and, in some cases, extremely dangerous pursuit. Syrian Christians have been suffering dreadfully during the current civil war, but believers in Israel have been offering financial and other support.

At the Crossroads, I pointed out in my opening pre-event fundraising article for potential supporters, is not about politics, but it *is* about a "peace process" as those attending will be exploring the degree to which faith in Jesus, the Jew, can break down centuries-old hostility and bring about dramatic harmony, affecting changes politicians and others have found impossible to achieve.

Among the speakers lined up was Canon* Andrew White, known as the Vicar of Baghdad. Canon Andrew has been working tirelessly in the field of reconciliation for years despite suffering from debilitating Multiple Sclerosis. In fact, he had just returned from the United States where he was honored with the 2014 William Wilberforce Award, presented by the Chuck Colson Center for Christian Worldview in recognition of his service to Christianity internationally and, in particular, in the Middle East.

Andrew has a huge congregation in the heart of war-torn Iraq and has lost many of his men to kidnapping and execution as the dust kicked up by Saddam Hussein's removal refuses to settle. And now it seems they are in more danger than ever under the reign of terror in the name of ISIS (Islamic State in Iraq and Syria). But he remains passionate about the Gospel's ability to heal wounds through the forgiveness and acceptance won for all on the cross. He was to tell his story at the conference, more on that and my interview with him later. I had already twice interviewed him over the phone but had never met him, so I was looking forward to seeing him in person.

An excellent opportunity for previewing *At the Crossroads* for media purposes came up back in March with a CMJ-sponsored day conference in Nottingham attended by a group of Iranian Christian refugees now attending various

* A title conferred on certain British clergymen as a special honor.

UK fellowships. They shared their vibrant testimonies and many indicated their desire to attend the Jerusalem gathering, prompting delegates to take up an offering to help them on their way.

Arriving in Israel for the Event

As we took off on El Al flight 318, I thought of how Israel had been re-born just a year before I came into the world on the slopes of Table Mountain in Cape Town, and I pondered on the somewhat enigmatic passage of Scripture in which Jesus (Yeshua in Hebrew) seemed to suggest that the generation who witnessed the re-birth of Israel would not pass away "until all these things were accomplished" presumably including the prophesied national recognition of Yeshua as Messiah. It proved to be one of those "goose-bump" experiences.

The Church, founded almost entirely by Jews, is now starting to re-connect with her roots and is witnessing a resurgence of so-called Messianic Jews (who believe Jesus is their Messiah), with congregations springing up in Israel and all over the world.

Yes, Israel is just 66 years young, but it is also 5,774 years old. Jewish people have been connected to this land for a very long time but, shortly after Jesus' miraculous, world-changing ministry on earth some 2,000 years ago, the Romans destroyed the country (just as Jesus foretold) which had the effect of dispersing God's chosen people to every corner of the globe—persecuted and bewildered and without a home.

But the prophets of old, like Isaiah, Jeremiah, and Ezekiel, promised that a time would come when they would be re-gathered to their ancient land—from the north, south, east, and west. It would be a twofold return, however, for once settled back in the land, they would also return to the Lord. Ezekiel writes about a "new heart"—a heart of flesh replacing a heart of stone (36:26). And Zechariah said there would come a time when they would look on "the one they have pierced" and mourn for Him as for an only child (12:10).

At the Crossroads, I wrote later, would witness something of this "new heart" as Jews reach out to their Arab brothers in love, humility, and concord. Here is a peace process lived out in action, not just in political talk. Here is a peace process that really *is* working!

I had a good flight, sitting next to a young mum with her gorgeous six-week-old baby girl, which meant I had extra leg room to allow for the cot to hang in front of us. And the little darling slept like a log, which helped me to catch a couple of hours dozing, ensuring that I didn't arrive in Tel Aviv quite so bleary-eyed as before. It's not an ideal time to fly, leaving at 10:30 p.m. and arriving at 3:30 a.m. (5:30 Israeli time), meaning that dinner is served around midnight. I took the shuttle bus for the 40-mile journey up to the heights of Jerusalem and, when dropped off in the bright, warm sunshine at 7:30, I felt a bit queasy at first from the effects of the driver weaving his "magic" through all those twists and turns up the mountains. But it was great to be back in beautiful Jerusalem, with the temperature around 25°C and climbing. I was also basking in the fantastic encouragement I had received throughout my journey from Linda, who texted me several times on her way back up north after dropping me off. We had spent a wonderful couple of days with my mum in London, culminating in a meal at an airport bar. And as I headed for customs, and found myself arriving in Israel on my own for the first time, I was more than a bit apprehensive. But I was much comforted by a text in which Linda said she felt that God had me "in a bubble" of protection—that there was nothing whatsoever to worry about, that He had it all sorted and I just had to trust implicitly in His leading.

One of my concerns had been on the technical front as to whether I would be able to connect successfully with the internet, without which my task could not be fulfilled. So one of the first things I did when I arrived at Christ Church was to hook up to the internet. And wallah! It worked a treat, even without a code as I emailed Linda to check she was receiving me loud and clear. I left my bags in reception until Don Stanley could take me up to where I would be staying with him and his wife, Caroline—in a spacious, modern apartment about a mile away. I had my own room and bathroom, and Don fixed me up perfectly with an internet code and even a British power platform for my plugs. With a desk in the corner, it was soon turned into a "news-room." Don is used to working with journalists, having spent years as a senior executive with both the BBC and the Australian Broadcasting Corporation, and effectively became my conference "editor," checking for nuances I might have overlooked and that sort of thing, which I found most helpful. Originally from Tasmania, Don and Caroline moved to Melbourne and, with their base now in Israel, it's obviously not easy being so far away from family and grandchildren. They were fabulous hosts and I became part of the family for a fortnight, feeling very much at home in their sixth floor flat (with two balconies) overlooking downtown Jerusalem. They both work incredibly hard, but I was glad to note that they too take the Sabbath seriously, putting their feet up and relaxing in style when it comes around. Having said that, there was a gravitas about Don which kept me on my toes. It wasn't for nothing that he had been a high-flyer in the media world. He's a no-nonsense character who, at the same time as being very gentle and loving, can be quite blunt and will tell you exactly what he thinks—whether responding to a piece of journalism or making an off-the-cuff comment. We share a love for cricket and for good British humor, of which his favorite are the *Two Ronnies*, and he delighted in sharing their DVDs with anyone who cared to watch. At one social gathering when he was about to upload an episode from the comedy duo, he turned aside to me with a mischievous look on his face, declaring, "I'm not sure if our American friends will get the humor. What do you think?" I told him to play it anyway as I knew he and I would be laughing our heads off in no time.

I spent much of my first afternoon talking with Paul Hames, who used to run the Christ Church center with his wife, Janey, and is now one of CMJ's key staff in England. We were then invited to a barbecue for conference workers but, as the number of guests kept rising, Paul was sent out to a local butcher's to stock up on meat, borrowing rector David Pileggi's car for the purpose. I accompanied him. We decided the meat needed washing down with something, so we also called in at a wine shop! And a long first day finished up in Rev. Pileggi's courtyard, overhung by jacarandas in blossom, as the conference treasurer, another Aussie, fanned the flames with some sort of petrol to the accompaniment of ominous thunder and lightning. And I learned that, though the conference was only days away, visas for a number of the delegates had yet to be approved!

Some of the guests had been negotiating with the Interior Ministry—always a delicate operation, but much more complicated now. We were trying to get entry permission for delegates from countries who were sworn enemies of Israel. Nothing about it was straightforward. "Why are they coming?" To those of us helping to organize the conference it was because they held the key to peace in the Middle East, but explaining that to government officials was another matter. A great deal of circumspection was required in trying to keep the delicate balance to which I've already referred. I think part of why it was proving more difficult to get visas for delegates than for the inaugural conference two years earlier was the very fact that we had made a decision to publicize what we were doing, even in advance. We had engaged in the really important business of correcting media bias and ignorance of the Middle East conflict. But of course such publicity was in itself fraught with risks.

It was a fun party nevertheless, though I could barely keep myself from falling asleep, and no one seemed to know where I fit into the overall picture. "Hi, I'm Paul," announced the genial Aussie, reaching out one hand as he stoked the barbecue with the other. "What's your role at the conference?" "Well, I guess I'm the communications man. I will be sending reports overseas." "Oh, I thought Steve (Carpenter) was doing that. Welcome anyway." And so it would go on until I wondered if I really did have a specific job. But I suppose it didn't matter, as long as God knew! It turned out the Steve referred to *was* in charge of liaising with the media, and of video production. But of course that was different from writing actual reports *for* the media. Anyway, it rained hard virtually all night and, although refreshed, I came around earlier than expected as the clanging, bell-type noise of the trams woke me up. The sound is used for a horn to warn pedestrians to get out of the way otherwise they're actually quiet.

Israel Fills the World with Fruit

I was afforded the huge privilege of visiting Israel in springtime. The colors of the flowering trees were magnificent, the sun was shining brightly and there was even the added blessing of abundant rain (very unusual at this time of year), though it would not have been welcomed by certain households who we could see from our sixth-floor bird's eye vantage point had chosen to ensure a cooler summer by taking tiles off their roofs in the mistaken belief that the rains were over.

All of this brings to mind the Scripture from the Book of Isaiah which says, "In days to come Jacob will take root, Israel will bud and blossom and fill all the world with fruit" (Isaiah 27:6).

Some 600 years later, Jesus indicated that the restoration of Israel (often symbolized by the fig tree) would be a sign that the end of the age was near. "When the fig tree blossoms, you know that summer is near," He said (Mark 13:28, paraphrased). The leaves and flowers contain the promise of the fruit to come.

The verse about fruit could be taken literally, of course, as Israel exports more than $2 billion worth of produce annually—tomatoes being its fourth largest commodity— and is among the world's top developers of better-looking, tastier, disease-resistant, and more nutritious varieties. And while Israeli agricultural teams continue to bring new fruit and vegetable varieties to the global market, we have God's promise of greater fruit to come—not of the natural, but of the supernatural type.

I have already mentioned Ezekiel's prophecy about the "new heart" Jews will experience and of how, in the words of Zechariah, there will come a time when they will recognize "the one they have pierced."

As their Foreign Affairs Minister, Avigdor Liberman says Israel itself is a miracle. Speaking at the start of my visit to Israel, on Independence Day on Tuesday May 6, he said, "Israel is a small country made up of people who returned after 2,000 years of exile from every corner of the earth to renew our sovereignty, many arriving straight from the hellish Holocaust, who had to fight for its very existence." And it has since become "one of the global powerhouses of hi-tech, innovation, energy and agriculture."

And while I must emphasize that neither the state nor individual Israelis are perfect, it is these amazing attributes that serve to prove God's Word is true: They are His chosen people, for better or for worse. They are as secular as other countries, but God still loves them, just as a father would not forsake a son who had gone astray.

Yet, with reference to Israel's 66th birthday, Mr. Liberman says it is time for clarity of vision, explaining how, while perfect vision is described in English as 20:20, the Hebrew way of saying it is 6:6, and in this respect it was essential to note that there was absolutely no desire for peace on the part of the Palestinians. Even the evacuation of 10,000 Jews from the Gaza Strip had not moved them one millimeter towards peace. On the contrary, they responded with 16,000 rockets and missiles. Nevertheless, Israel had always been a peace-seeking nation, he said, adding, "Israel wants an agreement, but we will not be fools."

The fig tree is blossoming; the fruit will come. But the Pharisees and Sadducees, who caused Jesus so much trouble when He walked these hallowed streets, are still around. Some Ultra-Orthodox Jews erect barricades around their suburbs in order to prevent potential Sabbath-breakers from entering their areas with cars or any such unholy thing. Worse than that, I'm told they organize protest marches and throw missiles at "renegades," necessitating the presence of riot police armed with water cannons—hardly an invitation to taste the delights of Judaism.

Let's face it, nor were the Crusades, pogroms, Spanish Inquisition, and the Holocaust—all linked in some way with Christianity—much of a shop window for persecuted Jews. But as I said, a good father will never turn his back on a prodigal son!

Peace in Our Time—in Jerusalem!

Meanwhile, I was writing daily online updates for *Israel Today*, a Jerusalem-based magazine, and various other publications, including a South African website called *Gateway News*. And as the stories began to make an impact, other outlets started picking them up. These included the *Times of Israel* and an American site called *World Net Daily*. It was time to write another article, this time in the form of a conference preview, which follows exactly as published:

> After yet another failure of Middle East talks,
> it would be perfectly understandable if claims
> of a successful peace process were met by gross

skepticism. But such a claim is being made, and it is very credible, judging by the evidence. I will explain in due course.

Following the breakdown of the latest US-sponsored Israeli-Palestinian negotiations aimed at securing some sort of deal, positions on both sides seemed to have hardened. The Israeli government is adamant they cannot do business with a Palestinian Authority now linked with terrorist group Hamas, who have vowed to destroy the Jewish state. And in any case the PA has shown no interest in peace by their constant refusal to recognize Israel's existence, which is to defy international agreements going back to the 1920s, quite apart from any Biblical claims.

And what hope is there of peace when Arab children are being taught—on television programs targeted at them, no less—to shoot "all the Jews," as the Palestinian Media Watch group shockingly revealed in their latest report? Their findings were based on the Hamas children's program, *Tomorrow's Pioneers*, screened on Al-Aqsa TV on May 2. And while PA leader Mahmoud Abbas declares that not a single Jew will be allowed in his proposed Palestinian state, the world's media accuses Israel of apartheid rather than their neighbors.

And yet, amidst all this conflict, a conference begins in Jerusalem tomorrow in which Arab and Jewish delegates will not be talking about peace, but living it out in action, embracing one another in the name of the Jew who changed the world, inaugurated a whole new era and who still brings peace to hearts all over the globe, including this strife-torn region.

The man who died a cruel death by being nailed to a Roman cross in this city 2,000 years ago has brought about this reconciliation between Arab and Jew, just as the Apostle Paul said it would, by breaking down "the dividing wall of hostility" through his sacrifice for sin.

Speaking of Jews and Gentiles, previously separated, he wrote, "His (Christ's) purpose was to create in himself one new man out of the two, thus making peace, and in this one body to reconcile both of them to God through the cross, by which he put to death their hostility." *(St Paul's Epistle to the Ephesians, chapter 2, verses 15 & 16)*

Called *At the Crossroads*, this unique invitation-only conference aims to deepen the bonds of fellowship between Muslim-background followers of Jesus and Jewish followers of Jesus as they encourage and support one another, thus making a significant contribution to real peace in the Middle East.

The conference will be held at Christ Church, just inside the magnificent walls of the Old City, and is part of a largely untold story of how Muslim-background Arab, Turkish, and Kurdish followers of Jesus from the Middle East and North Africa are forging close ties with Jewish believers in Jesus.

The organizers have taken inspiration from a Biblical passage in the Book of Isaiah (chapter 19), which speaks of a highway of blessing from Egypt to Assyria (which includes the Arab Middle East, north-western Iran, south-eastern Turkey, part of Armenia and Cyprus) via Israel. Delegates are coming from throughout the Middle East and North Africa.

The conference aims to strengthen a developing network of mutual co-operation and explore more practically how all the sons of

Abraham can together help build a "highway" of blessing in the region.[1]

After finishing the article, I joined other volunteers for a "chill-out" time, which is a monthly treat in which Don organizes a film showing with drinks and snacks provided. They also sing to anyone who has had a birthday that month and say goodbye (with gifts) to those who are leaving. But before the main feature, he showed some very funny clips from the *Two Ronnies* (a classic British comedy duo to which I have already referred) as a warm-up. The film itself, *One Chance*, was fabulous and is the true story of how opera star, Paul Potts, finally made it big despite the crushing blow of drying up in front of Pavarotti during a "master class" at the school he was attending in Italy.

---

1 Published in *Israel Today, Encounter Gospel News,* and *Gateway News,* May 12 and 14, 2014. See the Bibliography..

6

Crisis at the Customs

I woke up next morning (a Saturday, three days before the event) to the very disturbing news that nine of the Iranians who were coming to the conference from Britain had been sent back. I had met some of them at the one-day conference in Nottingham a couple of months earlier, and there seemed no doubt about the genuineness of their faith. What's more, they all had British passports. Don, my host and boss, initially informed me of the news over breakfast, saying they had turned up the previous night and had been immediately deported. Of course, this put a whole new slant on things, though the details were not as we had first heard. It turned out that five Iranians were being held at Tel Aviv's Ben Gurion Airport where they were being interrogated with a view to deportation. They ended up being held there for 48 hours before being sent on the next plane to London. However, one young lady was allowed through, for reasons we could never work out, and proved to be one of the stars of the conference. And her pastor, who was also to play an important part in the event, later followed her into the country and was waved through customs apparently unhindered. All of this presented me with a double dilemma: finding accurate information as to exactly what was happening, and knowing what to do with it.

As a veteran journalist of 40 years, it was an obvious story that I couldn't ignore, but at the same time, I was there as a servant of CMJ for the purpose of reporting on the conference itself, which was the best story of all because Arab and Jew were supposed to be in conflict with one another. But I needed to ensure the organizers were happy with me doing coverage of the deportations. In any case, I needed to elicit a comment from them about it. However, I could not at first contact them because they were conducting a pre-conference tour of Israel for some of the delegates. I managed to source various details as I bumped into people who seemed to know a little, but on the whole no one knew much, and I was getting progressively agitated—and I had been looking forward to a Sabbath rest!

I eventually managed to track down David Pileggi, who was happy for me to pen some kind of press statement for his perusal before sending out a report. In the end, he felt it would be better left unsaid, asking if I could hold onto the piece in case it was needed. My feeling, however, was that the story could well be the key to unlock the interest of the mainstream media, and as I explained, if it broke through some other means, the papers may well get the facts wrong and it would not be to our advantage. Better to be transparent and pre-empt any misconceptions that might result from a leak not coming from us.

Meanwhile, I had sent out texts and emails requesting urgent prayer from our UK intercessors. Unfortunately, my initial text to Linda was somewhat garbled and ambiguous in my obvious haste both to get the message out and restrict myself to 160 characters! The upshot of this was that the poor darling thought I too was coming home and was thus left distraught for the ensuing few hours as she contemplated the prospect of me being at the center of an international incident while suffering distress and humiliation in the process. She phoned me, panic-stricken and very upset, saying that she was confused, having received a text saying I was being asked to leave the country. Was it true? She had even called on the offices of a friend, Tom Chacko, a Revelation TV presenter with strong Israel sympathies, who had promised to phone the Israeli Embassy on our behalf.

It didn't at first occur to me that my text could have been misinterpreted, so I concluded that someone had hacked into my phone, and conspiracy theories took a new twist. I somehow managed to calm her down with assurances that I was not (as far as I knew) in trouble with the Israeli authorities and, after a bit of detective work from Don, concluded that she must indeed have misread my own text. I felt terrible, though relieved, to have put her through that. For her part, she felt an idiot, but it was my fault really. I'm always telling others to make themselves perfectly clear in emails as this kind of shortcut language is bound to confuse. And now my own sound advice had come back to bite me! The text actually said: "*Urgent prayer request. Need wisdom of Solomon; me & CMJ. 5 Iranians wi GB passports sent back. How 2 deal wi it?*" What I had meant was that both CMJ and myself needed the wisdom of Solomon in the case of five Iranians with British passports who were waiting to be deported. Oh dear! Please note, however, the crucial punctuation marks, which, if observed, make all the difference. English teachers are you listening?

Fortunately, Tom hadn't yet called the embassy. And as Linda later put it, "Lots of people have been praying for you and the situation who would not otherwise have been doing so, which means God must have wanted to mobilize them for a reason." And perhaps it was *this reason*, as I only learned much later, that the Iranian group being held at the airport were using their time there to tell all who would listen about the wonderful way in which Jesus had brought love, joy, and peace into their lives. Yes, even peace, amidst the tension and inconvenience of interrogation! On their return to Heathrow, they told of their disappointment at not seeing Jerusalem, but that it was more than made up by the opportunity of introducing two Muslim ladies to the love of Jesus! However, it was still a crisis and, though it didn't affect me in quite the same way, the issue remained a cause of personal tension for reasons already stated.

With the Lord's help, I managed to put my feelings aside about getting this particular story out and concentrate on the main issue of Jew and Gentile embracing one another. It was only later that I discovered that the story was effectively in the public domain by that time. Not only was it on the conference website, which I didn't even know existed until my stay was almost over, but the *Times of Israel* had also reported the affair on their site! So I might as well have put it out just as I had written it in the first place, thus:

UK-based Iranians Deported from Israel

Conference celebrating Arab-Jewish reconciliation hit by double blow

Five UK-based Iranians who are understood to have been granted asylum in Britain have been deported from Israel where they were hoping to attend a Christian conference.

Several Egyptian delegates have also been turned back at the border.

The Iranians were interrogated and held for 48 hours at Tel Aviv's Ben Gurion Airport and their case was eventually heard by a judge who, while apparently sympathetic, was swayed by a large file of evidence from the authorities that they posed an element of risk despite carrying British passports. Their UK citizenship is understood to have been acquired because their future in Iran was deemed unsafe in view of their Christian faith.

The invitation-only conference, called At the Crossroads, is being hosted by historic Christ Church in the heart of Jerusalem's Old City and starts today.

Arab Christians from all over the Middle East are meeting with Jewish followers of Jesus in a bid to deepen bonds of fellowship already established between them. And 120 delegates were originally invited.

They are coming from Jordan, Iraq, Turkey, and other countries in the region often perceived as enemies of Israel. But the participating Arabs, Turks, and Kurds have a view of Israel informed by a Christian faith solidly built on the Jewish Scriptures (Old Testament), and the conference organizers are encouraging further reconciliation.

Expressing huge disappointment at the deportations, Christ Church rector and conference spokesman Rev. David Pileggi said they had never had an incident like this in 200 years of being involved in Israel. (The church itself was built in the 1840s.)

Rev. Pileggi said, "We have been having people come over as our guests for years. But we do understand the security issues and we are not saying the immigration officials have got it wrong. We have also had amazing help and co-operation on other issues relating to this conference, for which we are very grateful, so we don't want to throw out the baby with the bathwater.

"But, yes, we're extremely disappointed and were so looking forward to having a full quota at this unique event, which can surely only serve to help ease tension and end conflict in this strife-torn region."

The conference organizers have taken inspiration from a Biblical passage in the Book of Isaiah (chapter 19), which speaks of a "highway" of blessing from Egypt to Assyria (which includes much of the Arab Middle East) via Israel.

Making More New Friends

My desk-in-a-corner "newsroom" and emailing network had already been used for urgent prayer requests for a Polish volunteer who had gone into labor too early and whose life was threatened. Thankfully she survived, but tragically the baby died. On a happier note, another news item sent was that a CMJ staff member's daughter got married amidst much celebration.

I smartened myself up for church on Sunday and drew a few oohs and aahs, especially from Americans, as everyone else is pretty casual. I told one delightful lady from Texas that I dress up, even for working at home, because I'm serving the King, which she thought was an interesting concept! But I do sometimes dress down. I even donned bright red shorts with my favorite check shirt when things got hotter.

A young American girl called Melissa, who turned out to be the conference administrator, said she had been plagued by fears about the situation in Israel as she flew over, but the Lord had encouraged her not to fear—that He had everything under control. These were among conversations I had after a magnificent worship service focused on unity and trusting in the Lord who is our Shepherd and the gate (or door) into life.

I had very tasty, generous, daily lunches at Christ Church as I caught up with old friends or made new ones. But sometimes I was treated to an extra main meal as Caroline—a former home economics teacher—served up some delectable dishes. I had many edifying chats with David Butterfield, husband of the new center manager Vida. It turned out we had much in common—he grew up in Zimbabwe, for one thing. And on my way home to the apartment that night I called in at Mike's Place, a lively bar on Jaffa Road, to quench my thirst. I duly got thoroughly engrossed with three young Jewish men, who were very open to spiritual things, especially the bartender. I'm sure it won't be long before Jews recognize their Messiah in big numbers. I also spoke much with an Irishman from Dublin, but he was actually quite aggressive and soon disappeared.

Anyway, the chap in charge asked me if I was interested in returning next day for their "Open Mic" evening. I told him I'd love to take part but hadn't brought my guitar with me. "Oh don't worry," he replied. "You can borrow mine!" I did return, and will tell all in a later chapter. It was an amazing experience—divine encounters the night before the conference.

I then discovered further connections of which I wasn't aware. Don and Caroline are close friends of Trevor and Margaret Davies, who are also well known to us. The couple first met as CMJ volunteers in 1999 when my hosts were in charge of Stella Carmel, the CMJ center near Haifa, as it was known then. The rule at the time was that staff/volunteer couples wishing to get married, as Trevor and Margaret did, had to ask permission of the director, Don, even though they were 53 and 45 respectively at the time. Margaret, who is Irish, was a good friend of Linda when they were both part of the community at the Christian Renewal Center in Rostrevor, Northern Ireland, very close to the border with Southern Ireland. And of course, that too was all about reconciliation—in Ireland's case across the Catholic-Protestant divide. Don and Caroline also know Cliff and Monica Hill, with whom I worked for years on a newspaper project which is yet to see fruition. Their daughter, Katherine, now living in England, was a volunteer for a time at Moggerhanger Hall in Bedfordshire where the Hills were based for many years.

Meanwhile, Linda was busy trying to book a suitable cottage in which to celebrate our anniversary for a few days shortly after I got back, sending over a selection of beautifully peaceful and charming venues in various nooks of the Yorkshire Dales which we love so much. We eventually agreed upon Stable Cottage on a farm close to Robin Hood's Bay, to which we have returned every year since our honeymoon in 2001. The stunning scenery in this area cannot be bettered, I'm sure, outside of heaven, and it's all so romantic.

So I had much to look forward to following my hectic schedule in Jerusalem! I had been feeling stressed and had suffered an all-day headache, which even two Panadols failed to remove, which is most unlike me. As ever, Linda was full of encouragement, writing: "God has called you and will give you everything you need at this time to fulfill His plans and purposes."

Christ Church, Old City Jerusalem

7

The Real Middle East
Peace Process

So it is that, amidst the turmoil of the Middle East with virtual civil wars erupting all around, a remarkable peace process was taking place in which Arabs, Jews, and Christians were embracing one another in the name of Jesus.*

As part of an ongoing spread of the Gospel in this volatile part of the world, *At the Crossroads* was held to inspire pastors and other leaders from the region who have discovered that Christ is the ultimate reconciler and that the "Prince of Peace" holds the key to a stable future in the area. The event was scheduled for May 13-16, Tuesday evening to Friday evening, with morning, afternoon, and evening meetings Wednesday to Friday. It was held in Christ Church, a beautiful 165-year-old building within the walls of Jerusalem's Old City.

I have to confess that before the conference officially started (it *was* an evening session), I met up with my friend Keren Pryor (widow of well-known Hebraic roots teacher, Dwight) at the Dublin Bar, where a liter (not just a pint) of Guinness provided ample fuel for the journey ahead!

---

* In chapters 7, 8, and 9, unless otherwise stated, the sections consist of previously published articles written by the author about the *At the Crossroads* event, reworked and, in some cases, re-titled for this book. See the Bibliography.

I was so glad when the conference finally got underway that evening, and it was all I hoped it would be, and more! This was clearly something very special. The presence of God was tangible, and there was an expectancy among the hushed congregation of something truly awesome about to take place. And yet there was no big fanfare, glitz, or hype. Opening the conference, Christ Church rector David Pileggi said, "It was always the vision that this church should actually be a refuge for the people of Israel and a place where the nations find healing."

David was calmness personified as he warmly welcomed all the delegates—or at least all who had managed to make it through customs. A big man with a mop of curly hair and a broad smile, he gives the impression of being completely unruffled despite the organizational rollercoaster ride from which he had just emerged. His quiet, yet firm, leadership certainly injected an added sense of peace to the whole event, and we were soon somewhat lost in the wonder of praise as the musicians struck up on piano, guitar, and keyboard. Their skills were undeniable, but it was especially moving to hear how our voices blended into a heavenly-sounding chorus, even though some were clearly unfamiliar with the language. We sang, alternatively, in English, Hebrew, Arabic, Turkish, and Farsi as the words were projected onto a screen. Those like me who were unfamiliar with most of the various languages did their best to follow the words at least phonetically.

Thus I was surrounded by men and women from many nations, most of whom could not speak my language. But we knew we were family worshipping a common Father, the King of Kings and Lord of Lords. We somehow understood each other: that we were brothers and sisters belonging to Jesus—Yeshua in Hebrew and Yesu in Farsi! And so throughout many heart-thumping moments of sheer joy and exhilaration, I witnessed the breaking down of barriers which St. Paul describes as the effect of the cross of Christ, "His purpose was to create in himself one new man out of the two, thus making peace, and in this one body to reconcile both of them to God through the cross, by which he put to death their hostility" (Ephesians 2:15-16).

Israel and Iran Pray for Each Other

It was especially moving to witness a profound gesture of peace between Israel and Iran as the event gathered momentum.

The UK-based Iranian pastor who successfully made it through customs was among those present. But when a conference organizer reminded his audience that Iran had not always been a sworn enemy of Israel vowing to destroy them—in fact, they used to be allies—he took the opportunity to pray a blessing over that country, asking God to re-open the gates between them so they would once more be friends.

This pastor, Youhana Darvishi,* then returned the favor by praying a blessing over Israel.

Another conference spokesman said many had paid a high price for attending. Indeed, it was at risk to their lives in some cases as Christians are undergoing tremendous persecution in a number of Muslim-background countries.

The previous—and inaugural—*At the Crossroads* event in 2012 has already borne much fruit as those who attended began to help each other in various ways. One Israeli believer

---

* *not his real name as requested for security reasons*

put his life on the line no less than 30 times in order to bring aid to suffering Christians in Syria.

Reuven Berger, pastor of a Hebrew congregation meeting at Christ Church on Saturdays, reminded his hearers that "Abraham loved Ishmael very much" and that God promised a blessing to Ishmael as well as Isaac, from whom the Jews are descended. Reuven's parents, respectively German and Austrian, managed to flee the Nazis in 1938, but his grandparents were sadly trapped in Europe and murdered. He said, "We are seeing more and more people from a Muslim background receiving the faith of Jesus, the Messiah. God is bringing Isaac and Ishmael together..."

Another delegate reported on rapid church growth in Algeria which had started in the late 1990s with many people having visions of Jesus. Whole villages are being converted in some cases, and it was like walking through the pages of the Book of Acts with healings and other miraculous manifestations taking place. And the believers there were now reaching out to other countries.

For me, a chance meeting over lunch summed up what the conference is all about. David Milburn, 54, a Jewish Israeli originally from Hendon in north London, was in charge of the technical side of the event, and recently married Annie, a 30-year-old Armenian Arab. As a couple, they felt called to be a role model of Middle East reconciliation. "We see this as our life-calling—God enabling us to live out the life of Christ, who breaks down every barrier," David explained. And they have now had an addition to the family—baby Amie.

Another work of compassion crossing the political and cultural divide also featured at the conference involves a Christian ministry called Shevet Achim. They rescue children with life-threatening heart conditions from surrounding Arab countries and provide them with the best possible treatment at top Israeli hospitals. Spokesman Jonathan Miles said, "So many people are ready to receive the message of reconciliation with Israel."

Iran's Gospel Revolution

I had already met the aforementioned British-based Iranian pastor Youhana Darvishi in Nottingham and was thrilled that, despite the difficulties experienced by his compatriots, he had made it to the conference.

Coming from a nation whose leaders have vowed to destroy Israel, Youhana now leads an Iranian church in the UK and has said that, despite the Islamic revolution of 1979 which closed doors to missionaries, the number of believers in his country has since grown exponentially from a mere 2,000 to around one million!

Speaking in Farsi, interpreted by a member of his congregation, he said, "They thought it was all over—that Jesus was dead. Pastors were murdered and there was no more printing of Bibles. It was like the disciples must have felt after Jesus was crucified. But God made a way where it seemed there was no way."

Youhana became a Christian at the age of six after viewing a TV program he believes was being screened to show Jesus in a negative light.

It was an excerpt from the film *Jesus of Nazareth* that really grabbed his attention. Jesus was being flogged and hauled before the Roman governor Pontius Pilate at His mock trial, and Youhana recalled, "I fell in love with this person. I told my mum, 'I love Him.'"

As a result, his mother took a risk by going out to find a VHS video (illegal in Iran at the time) about Jesus. "I watched it every week and started writing down all the dialogue of that movie, which became my Bible, as I didn't have one. God will find a way, even for a six-year-old boy."

Jesus Reconciles Muslim Couple

It was amazing how much of an impact the Iranians made in spite of having had most of their contingent deported! Esther Esfahani,* the young lady who was mysteriously allowed through customs while her compatriots were sent back to Britain, managed to recover from her harrowing ordeal to such an extent that she ended up sharing one of the most powerful testimonies of the conference. And though she does speak a little English, she chose to share her story in Farsi, which was duly translated.

Brought up as a devoted Muslim, she told how she became a Christian after an encounter with the God of the Bible. I have not used her real name for security reasons as the Iranian government not only persecutes Christians but has also vowed to destroy Israel.

Shortly after moving to England some years ago, Esther started a coffee shop and took on some Christian staff. But she left strict instructions that they were not to talk about their faith. On her day off, her husband, who worked elsewhere, took care of the shop and one day she noticed a book about Christianity on top of the dishes, which made her very angry. It turned out that her husband had decided to follow Jesus, but at this stage she refused to delve further into the book. She said, "I had this idea that if you're a Muslim and

---

* *not her real name*

you accept another religion something bad will happen to you."

Two weeks later she saw a Bible in the shop. "I got so angry I kicked out the Christian staff and initiated divorce proceedings against my husband—we had been married 19 years."

She wasn't just a committed follower of Islam—she had actually taught the Koran. "So I told him I could not be with him any longer if he was now a Christian. But the angrier I became, the calmer he grew. He was being so kind. So to prove Islam is better I started to read more of the Koran and wrote down what was either good or interesting. But then I discovered things that weren't so good, like all this about cutting hands and taking multiple wives. So I decided not to read it anymore, but still wanted to divorce my husband.

"So I went to inform my sister about this, only to find that she too had become a Christian! And a little later, when my husband was away, she suggested we watch a movie together. It was all about Jesus, and I was so angry that people opposed Him when He had done so many good things. Then suddenly I heard a voice saying, 'You are just the same! You are watching this, but cannot believe it.' I looked around to see who was speaking, but there was no one there.

"I subsequently got quite depressed because I didn't have any kind of relationship with God and after all these years was suffering at the hands of my husband. So when my sister took a shower, I secretly picked up her Bible and started to read it. Eventually I prayed, 'If You're real and alive, can You start speaking to me as You speak to them?'

"And that evening I opened the Bible at random (as Muslims do with the Koran) and it fell open at Revelation (the last book of the New Testament). My eyes were drawn to the words of Jesus, which said, 'Here I am! I stand at the door and knock. If anyone hears my voice and opens the door, I will come in and eat with him, and he with me' (Revelation 3:20).

"I was so afraid I was shaking. So I closed the book but then opened it again at the very same place, at which point I just fell down and said, 'OK, You are God; I want to accept You!'

"Next day I was crying when I called my husband, who at first misunderstood as he pleaded for me to give him another chance. But I told him that, when he came home, I wanted to read the Bible with him and together commit our way to Jesus. By this time he too was crying as he thanked God for answering his prayers.

"When he returned, my heart had been totally changed and I was in love with my husband. My two sons noticed the difference in our lives and how Jesus had brought peace out of conflict, and now all our family are serving God in church."

Esther finished by praying for all Iranians, and saying she believes the gift of God her family has experienced is also available to all Muslims.

Jesus Answers Call for Help from Muslim

I was privileged in between my trips to Israel to hear the testimony of another Iranian living in Britain. Also once a devoted Muslim, Fereydon Taghipour-Khankahdani had tried his best to follow the strict rules of his faith, but when he was starving to death as he slept rough in the snow of a European winter, it was no help to him.

"I was running away from the eyes of the Iranian police, as I had challenged the nature of the revolution there when I returned to my country after years of living in Dubai. Now I'm a British citizen. This country saved my life. But it was Jesus who opened the door."

In Dubai he had been a well-paid fashion photographer working with beautiful girls for top brands like Chanel. But the lavish lifestyle he experienced there doesn't begin to compare with the joy of the relationship he now has with God. He has never been happier, and there's nowhere he'd rather be.

Early in Fereydon's 16-year stay in Dubai, he worked in a picture frame shop where, despite the owner being a Muslim, there was a copy of the well-known poem, "Footprints in the Sand," which talks about how, when we walk with God, there are two sets of footprints, but when things get really tough, there is just one—because it is at those times that Jesus is carrying us on His shoulders.

"I wondered what it meant. I couldn't understand it. I was born a Muslim and kept the Sharia Law (a strict code of ethics) as much as possible to try to get close to God, which never happened. I found that, in just one minute, I committed ten sins and that it was impossible to be pure like God. Now I know that's why He provided a way through Jesus, His Son, who acted as a bridge connecting us to God.

"I could not jump across this deep chasm until Jesus— 'the way, the truth, and the life'—carried me. I believed in God as a young child and was always seeking Him. I knew there was a life apart from what we were experiencing now, which was just temporary. But in my mind, God was very judgmental—someone waiting to strike me with a stick if

I committed sin. But it was impossible to get close to Him. He was only there to punish me, not to encourage me like a father.

"I couldn't see any love in Islam. What I saw was blood and hate, revenge and retaliation. If I got to heaven, I would only qualify to live with the animals. Then, when I had 'issues' with the government of Iran, I fled to Europe with the ultimate intention of joining up with my brother in Canada.

"I travelled all over Europe seeking refuge and for six long months I was in a very bad situation. It got to the point where I was reduced to skin and bone, and I couldn't go any further. I was about to kill myself when, one night in the middle of the bushes in the freezing snow, I shouted out to God for help.

"I had been reduced to eating paper to survive as I slept most nights out in the open over a six-month period when I'm not even sure whether I was in Belgium or France."

On the verge of suicide, he asked God to show himself as he prayed in the name of Mohammed, but there was no answer. He then prayed in the name of Ali followed by Fatima, other Islamic leaders, but still he found no release from his suffering.

Finally, he asked if God could help him because of Jesus, and a miracle happened. "Within two days all my issues were sorted out and I was in the UK where I was accepted as a refugee," he told me in Doncaster, South Yorkshire, where he now lives.

"Islam had no answer, and it was as if JESUS was the code to opening the door for me. He hadn't come to judge me, but to help me. He didn't come to show off, but to meet my needs. It was a revolution in my life. And when I joined the Christians in Doncaster, I noticed how they had a wonderful relationship with Jesus in the way they worshipped and with how they could talk to Him in private, and He would listen.

"When I got baptized it was snowing outside—reminding me of when I first met Jesus in my great desperation—and, as the snowflakes came down, I felt like it was my wedding day. I was walking on air!

"Now I put my trust absolutely in God, who gives me everything I need both materially and spiritually. I am literally basking in the blessing of God. I thought the life I had in Dubai was good, but I was really sinking into the darkness. Though glamorous on the surface, it was empty underneath."

The 45-year-old is now a third-year student at Mattersey Bible College in nearby north Nottinghamshire. He also preaches and helps to run services at his church, an outreach to the Iranian community by the Methodists of Hexthorpe, near the town center.

Fereydon speaks four languages—Farsi, Arabic, English and Urdu—and is proud of his Persian heritage, particularly with the exchange of cultures that has evolved over the centuries between Persia and Israel.

The ancient Persian King Cyrus, for example, though head of a great empire, had submitted himself to the "God of Israel" in agreeing to let the Jewish exiles return to their homeland from Babylon.

Fereydon adds that most of Iran's people do not share the anti-Israel sentiments of their government, who have repeatedly stated their intention to wipe the Jewish state off the map. "I love Israel," he says, "and the Jewish people are very nice. I met some of them in Antwerp. I would love to go to Israel when I get the chance and share in the 'highway of love' the prophet talks about in Isaiah 19 when Arab and Jew would embrace each other all the way from Egypt to Assyria (including part of modern-day Iran and Syria)."

8

Muslim Finds Jesus in Mecca!

If the previous story doesn't strike you as divine intervention, then try to get your head around this one shared at the conference: A Turkish Muslim who made a pilgrimage to Mecca in a desperate attempt to get his life back on track returned as a Christian to the great astonishment of his family.

Now pastor of a church in the Turkish capital of Ankara, Ali Pektash sees it as part of his mission to help re-unite the sons of Abraham. Ali, a Kurd, was a wife-beater who suffered from alcohol addiction when friends persuaded him to make Hajj (pilgrimage) to Islam's holy city. It is in Saudi Arabia, where liquor is banned, and the religious ritual might cure him, they suggested.

When he got there, he cried out to God for help and fell asleep. Jesus then appeared to him in a dream and touched him, saying, "You believe in Me now; leave this place."

After taking a shower the next morning, he discovered what he thought was dust on the part of his chest Jesus had touched, but, in fact, the dark hair on his chest had turned white in the shape of a hand!

At the traditional celebration marking his return from Hajj, he announced to his incredulous family that he had seen Jesus in Mecca and had come back a Christian.

He burst out crying in front of his wife and asked forgiveness for the way he had treated her, clearly demonstrating a dramatic change in his life. For three years he had no access to a Bible and it was seven years before he met another Turkish Christian.

He eventually started a church in Ankara, which he has recently handed over to trusted elders in order to begin a new work in Eastern Turkey, where he was raised.

Robert Sakr, one of the visionaries behind the conference who is based in Beirut, Lebanon, and who knows Ali personally, pointed out that in that society you don't admit to having made a mistake, especially where they kill "apostates"—those who have converted from Islam to Christianity.

He said he finally plucked up the courage to ask Ali what he had been talking about all those years (before he found a Bible and fellow Christians). And his reply was, "I told them how I was a wife-beater and abused alcohol, and that Jesus has delivered me!"

And wasn't he in danger of capital punishment for turning away from Islam? "No," he replied. "They slaughtered a sheep in my honor because they remembered who I was. And if I could be so changed, they weren't going to touch me with a bargepole."

Robert eventually had the gall to ask to see Ali's chest. "He took his shirt off for me, and I saw the snow-white handprint against his black hair."

Although he grew up in Israel with missionary parents, Robert was not impacted by the Gospel until he heard a visiting Arab evangelist, and that changed his life forever. Now he says, "More Muslims have come to Christ in the last four years than in the previous 400."

Speaking in Turkish (translated through headsets for those who needed it), Ali told the conference how Abraham was also *his* ancestor, and how he saw it as part of his mission to help re-unite the children of Isaac and Ishmael (Abraham's sons by different wives).

Illustrating how family division can cause lasting conflict among the children affected, he said it was no different for the descendants of Abraham who continue to be embroiled in much strife and contention with each other. But now it was time for reconciliation. "We have a very important ministry—to reconcile the world," he said. But it could only be done through Jesus. "Everybody in Turkey says they believe in God," he said. "But people are persecuting me!"

In a further example of reconciliation, a Palestinian delegate from Hebron (where Abraham is buried) said, "I was one of those who hated the Jews, but Jesus changed my life." A number of Israeli pastors responded by laying hands on him in prayer and offering words of encouragement.

Speaking for myself, I was profoundly moved when, during a communion service the previous night, I was surrounded by a Turk, Egyptian, Iranian, Armenian, and an Israeli originally from South Africa. Although there was a language barrier in some cases, we embraced each other without words during the traditional "peace" greeting that immediately precedes the sharing of bread and wine.

9

From Baghdad to Jerusalem

After submitting those articles on the opening of the conference, my next assignment, clearly, was to report that the Vicar of Baghdad had come to Jerusalem to encourage Middle East nations to join the highway of blessing through a conference aimed at cementing bonds of reconciliation between Jew and Gentile.

I met the honored Canon Andrew White over lunch, reminding him that I had interviewed him twice before at length over the phone. Standing very tall and slightly unsteadily—he suffers from Multiple Sclerosis—he is an imposing, larger-than-life figure in more ways than one. Often joking and with a sort of permanent twinkle in his eye, his booming foghorn voice lets everyone know he's coming, and he is clearly little concerned about what people think. And yet for someone so obviously blunt and undiplomatic, he commands huge respect among politicians and others in the Middle East. That is not to say he doesn't have a price on his head, too. And I suppose that's it, really. He is secure in who he is and what he is called to do, and is concerned only about living for his Lord.

The conversation soon got around to the deportations, which immediately prompted him to ask (loudly) why they (the conference organizers) hadn't asked for his help. He knew the Israeli Prime Minister personally and could easily have sorted it all out. And if I understood him correctly, I think Youhana, the Iranian pastor, was later let through because of Andrew's intervention as, when he heard that the pastor had returned to Britain to fulfill another engagement, he sounded distinctly put out. "What?! I persuaded Binyamin Netanyahu to let him into the country, and he's already gone back?!"

I had been told to expect a retinue of bodyguards in his wake, but I couldn't see anyone who might have fit the bill, although perhaps that was because they were so well disguised. But he did have a very attractive young PA, Vanessa, who was most helpful as she answered a number of questions I had. She was quite concerned about his lack of appetite. She said he ate less than a child's portion. She didn't know how he managed to do all he does with so little nourishment. He took ages just to get through a bowl of soup over lunch, which was apparently all he needed. He then invited me to join them on a trip to Bethlehem that afternoon. With a perfectly straight face, he said they were going to see Joseph, the carpenter! Of course, I thought he was joking, but he wasn't. Apparently, this particular Joseph does beautiful wood carvings. Anyway, it was a very kind offer, and it seemed a bit churlish of me to turn it down, but in all honesty I did have work to do along with an appointment to which I was committed, and we wouldn't have been back in time.

Andrew leads a 6,500-strong congregation at St. George's in the heart of war-torn Baghdad. He told the conference how his people were happy despite much suffering—1,276 of them have perished as victims of violence in the past ten years.

But Iraq has a Christian heritage going back to ancient times, he explained, and was part of the "Isaiah 19 Highway" which forms the vision of the conference. The highway, remember, speaks of how Egypt, Israel, and Assyria (comprising much of the Middle East) will one day be a blessing to each other.

White's entire congregation originates from Nineveh in northern Iraq, where the prophet Jonah reluctantly preached after being swallowed by a whale, and where "Doubting Thomas" brought the message of the risen Jesus 700 years later. But Iraqi Christians are now paying a heavy price for their faith, yet they soldier on undaunted. Asked how they could all be so happy when things were so awful, one of Andrew's adopted daughters replied, "When you've lost everything, Jesus is all you've got."

He said Iraq formed the northern part of the highway described by Isaiah as God's "handiwork." And he revealed that representatives of Christ Church had been responsible for founding St. George's in 1864, so the link today was highly appropriate.

Now traveling about at great risk and with the added discomfort of suffering from MS, he has a great love for Jews as well as Muslims and has spent some time in Israel, including a spell as the only Gentile ever to attend an Ultra-Orthodox school there. Every week in his church they begin their service by singing the Shema, the ancient Hebrew declaration of worship for the one true God.

He pointed out that the "Isaiah 19 Highway" was particularly significant in that it represents all the places through which Abraham travelled—and he is the father of both Arab and Jew.

His church, closed by Saddam Hussein in 1991 when the Americans and British began bombing Baghdad, was re-opened in 2003 without a stick of furniture except for the dictator's "throne." Initially peopled mainly by diplomats and military staff, it emptied out when the country started getting really dangerous, at which point Iraqis began attending. And it grew exponentially in spite of the carnage.

He told some extraordinary stories. Faced with a famine at one point, the Grand Ayatollah of Iraq came to ask if he would pray as there was no food in the country. The vicar had just $12 in his pocket but, presumably mindful of the feeding of the 5,000 with just five loaves and two fish and because he had no intention of offending the Ayatollah, he prayed. As a result—and apparently without any money being exchanged—thousands of tons of meat were delivered to his premises and 50 refrigerated lorries were laid on to distribute it all over the country.

Canon White said he had seen the glory of God in Iraq. On visiting the shrine of the prophet Ezekiel, located in an ancient oriental synagogue-turned-mosque, he saw an angel standing at each corner, and has seen angels every single day since. "When they killed 58 of our church people one day, there were angels all around the funeral cars."

He said the glory of God was coming from the East, just as Ezekiel had foretold in chapter 43 of the book named after him, and it was returning to Jerusalem.

As mentioned, Andrew had just returned from America where he picked up the 2014 William Wilberforce Award, presented for his efforts at reconciliation by the Chuck Colson Center for Christian Worldview. He has been used much as a hostage negotiator and, though reared in the (Pentecostal)

Assemblies of God, he says he was called into the Church of England for a purpose that only became clear later when he found himself engaged in the work of reconciliation—a ministry facilitated by his Anglican standing.

He has been forced by death threats to flee Iraq in the past, only succumbing to the pressure of "Wanted: dead or alive" posters in order to protect the hostages whose release he had been negotiating in a country still beset by sectarian strife and in danger of being overrun by jihadists (Islamic warriors). As I write, he is understood to have temporarily relocated to Bethlehem due to a £36 million bounty placed on his head by the Islamic State (ISIS) terrorists. In a recent tour of the USA raising funds for impoverished Christians suffering in Iraq, he told of the horrors of children being chopped in half by ISIS. His church has been deprived of many of its men through killings and kidnappings, and he is also "daddy" to many of the children who have been orphaned as a result. In my interview with him several years ago, he said, "I have regularly been held at gunpoint, thrown into rooms with chopped off bits of body and received death threats, many coming because of my involvement in hostage negotiations."

It was during his time in Kennington, London, some 25 years ago that someone shared a "picture" she had received from God of Canon White in "a very hot country." But he wanted to stay in England and be a vicar in London with a hospital chaplaincy.

He did not even start off wanting to be a minister. His one desire was to work in the field of anesthetics, so he trained to be an operating department practitioner at St. Thomas' Hospital in London where he worked after qualifying. Then one night as he was praying in the hospital garden, just opposite Big Ben, he heard the Lord say he must go into the church—and specifically the Church of England (C of E).

He was not impressed. Although attending an Anglican church, he wasn't even a member of the C of E. "I was reared in the Assemblies of God (AOG) and my grandfather was an AOG missionary and assistant to the legendary Smith Wigglesworth, whose Bible was passed on to me. I grew up on stories of Smith, Donald Gee, Howard and John Carter. To me the C of E wasn't even really very Christian. But I gave in to God and realize now that if I had not joined the Anglican Church, I would not even be here in Iraq."

So he studied theology at Cambridge and was then literally "sent to Coventry," where he became canon of the cathedral there. He took on the responsibility for the International Center for Reconciliation at the then *new* Coventry Cathedral, which rose from the ashes after being destroyed by the Germans in World War II—hence the focus on reconciliation with old enemies.

Of Iraq, he says: "It is the most wonderful nation in the world. God must like it too as this is where creation began in the Garden of Eden, and where salvation history started with the birth of Abraham in Ur. It is also where the greatest mission in history took place, though admittedly led by the most miserable evangelist ever—Jonah. He did not want to come here, but eventually arrived via submarine transportation in Nineveh, which to this day is mainly Christian and most of my Iraqi congregation come from there."

I must say I felt honored to have finally met Canon White, and will be praying for him all the more in light of the ominous developments in Iraq. Sadly, because of the horrific danger, he was forced to stay away from Iraq completely. He says all the Christians have had to flee and thousands have been slaughtered.[1] So, now he has turned his attention to helping the Iraqi refugees in Jordan.[2]

A Highway to Welcome Jesus Back!

A feature of the conference that warmed the hearts of all was Israelis, Palestinians, and Egyptians praying for and embracing one another. Delegates rejoiced when hearing of a recent youth conference in Israel at which Jewish, Arab, and Palestinian young people came together for three days of worship, which an Archbishop in the region had described as "the real peace process in the Middle East."

Our conference worship was another foretaste of heaven as glorious songs of praise—in Turkish, Hebrew, English, Farsi, and Arabic—were accompanied by the aforementioned skillful musicians. And, with some sessions open to the public, many nations from beyond the region joined the delegates. At one stage, dozens of individuals representing different countries took it in turn to praise God in their own language. And it was exciting for me as a South African to hear a visitor from Cape Town praying in Afrikaans.

As with Canon White, a preacher from Singapore also spoke about the glory of God coming from the East. But Dr. George Annadorai was thinking of countries much further out than Iraq, and told the conference that we may well

---

1 Andrew White being interviewed on Nov. 6, 2014 about the dangers in Iraq: https://www.youtube.com/watch?v=fiB7nEw YJNg&noredirect=1

2 Andrew White's website news: http://frrme.org/news/

be living in the generation to witness Jesus' return, which echoed thoughts I was having as I took off from Heathrow.

The "Isaiah 19 highway" would pave the way for that event just as John the Baptist had prepared the way for the Messiah's first coming. George spoke of the convergence of this road with another highway from the East, all the way to China and Japan, from whence the last major move of God would sweep all before it on the way back to Jerusalem.

The ancient religions of the world had all originated in the East, representing most of the world's population (five billion people) and where idol worship now predominates, whereas ideology had become the god of the West, he explained, adding that Israel had an association with the East going back 3,000 years to the time of King Solomon, for which there is strong evidence—and the Solomon Islands is just one example. Ezekiel, as I have mentioned, talks of the glory of God coming from the East in advance of the Messiah's return, and of course the Wise Men came from the East.

Citing the "Back to Jerusalem" movement of Chinese Christians taking the message of Jesus back to where it all began, George said that though this was good, God would not allow them to do it on their own. "No one person is allowed to carry the ark (representing the presence of God)," he said. As it happens, a new highway to Jerusalem is currently under construction at great expense as huge mechanical diggers cut their way through the steep slopes ascending Mount Zion.

News Spreading

My reports were now going to four continents—Israel, South Africa, Britain, and the United States, the latter added after David Pileggi told me that *Christianity Today* (the American magazine) were keen for coverage. So *Hallelujah* was in order, and it was echoed by a street performer singing the Leonard Cohen version of the song on my way up to my "news-room." Yet still I felt lots of tension, which was perhaps not too surprising in the circumstances as a mighty spiritual battle was obviously being waged over the "air-waves"—and Jerusalem was the epicenter of it all.

Yes, it's the most beautiful place on earth, but it was like being on a roller-coaster. One minute you're on top wondering if you could cope with any more excitement, and the next you're getting all worked up over various issues. I started to feel quite shattered and emotionally drained and finding that I was virtually meeting myself coming back as I continually tried to catch up on writing assignments. There was a sense at times that I longed to get back on "terra firma," back to normality and in the loving arms of my wife instead of this constant whizzing around in head-spinning mode. Yet I loved being there all the same, making the most of every moment, catching the relatively cool Jerusalem breeze in my face and breathing deeply of its warmth and vibrancy.

Turning to romance, I was delighted to learn of the engagement of my niece whose boyfriend had gotten down on one knee to propose by the lake at Virginia Water in Surrey. She apparently thought it was a joke, just laughing and not replying for what seemed ages. I was also warmed by news that the sun had finally decided to make an appearance back in England, and that Linda was contemplating spending time in the garden, which she loves doing.

As I love to do, being a marathon runner, I went on several runs, which proved a marvelous way to blow off the cobwebs that had built up while hunched over my laptop screen. There's no better way to tour the city, except that much patience is required waiting for the green pedestrian light when crossing busy roads. My most memorable run was to the top of the Hebron Road, three miles away, and up onto the newly-constructed "Peace Forest" promenade.

On the reporting front, I was much encouraged by another chance conversation over lunch with David Milburn, whom I have already mentioned, the Jewish Israeli, originally from London, in charge of all things technical at the conference. He felt moved to pray over me after I shared my vision for a national newspaper reporting and interpreting from a Biblical worldview. He felt very strongly that it was of God and prayed all kinds of relevant Scriptures, which I have been given over the years, and that the machinery would start rolling towards launch. It was an emotional encounter and an encouragement back in Britain for Carole Heath, an intercessor who has supported me with the vision for a number of years.

I made another visit to the Anglican International School on Prophets Street, just around the corner from the Stanley apartment, and caught up with Lawrence Hilditch, the new head from Belfast, as well as outgoing head Owen Hoskin, who was soon to be returning to New Zealand and who gave me a wonderful idea for a novel which I hope to start working on soon! I was also very grateful for the help given by Carino Casas, a Christ Church-based photographer from Texas, who supplied me with several pictures when I didn't have anything suitable for my articles. She's very professional and has all the fancy equipment (especially for indoors and for doing hi-tech things like blurring out faces, which was sometimes necessary). Having said that, my Smartphone worked very well as a camera and I took some excellent outside photos which even impressed Erin Georgiou, editor of South Africa's *Joy* magazine who had commissioned me to write a 1,500-word double-page spread including pictures. Joy (also known as *Jeug)* publishes in both English and Afrikaans and is the biggest circulation Christian magazine outside the United States!

10

Palestinian's Recipe for Peace

One of those scheduled to speak, but who unfortunately had to cancel at the last minute for some reason, was Taysir "Tass" Saada, a former assassin and personal chauffeur to the late PLO leader Yasser Arafat.

Naturally, we were all disappointed he couldn't make it, but I knew something of his story from reports of what he said at the 2012 *At the Crossroads* conference and from reading his book, *Once an Arafat Man*.[1] Tass once had Israeli soldiers in the sights of his rifle. But now he loves Jews and spends all his time promoting reconciliation.

Tass was born in Gaza shortly after the founding of modern Israel. He grew up, as many other Muslims did, with hatred in his heart for the people he accused of stealing Arab land. His parents ran a business in Jaffa, near Tel Aviv, before taking refuge in Gaza in the wake of warnings to Arab residents from neighboring countries intent on snuffing out the new Jewish state at birth.

They later moved to Saudi Arabia and Qatar, but Tass joined the PLO (Palestine Liberation Organization) while still a teenager and contributed to a historic victory over the Israelis in a surprise attack on the east side of the Jordan.

---

1 Tass Saada with Dean Merrill, *Once an Arafat Man,* Tyndale Publishing, 2008.

However, he became a wanted man in Jordan after trying to assassinate their Crown Prince, but hitting the wrong car.

He ended up in America where he found success in the restaurant business after being allowed to stay through what began as a marriage of convenience to Karen, who already had a baby son. They later had a daughter together, but the relationship came under severe strain as work demands took Tass away for long periods. Then one day a loyal, long-term customer, challenged him with the extraordinary statement: "If you want the peace I have, you must love a Jew!"[2]

Charlie Sharpe, a wealthy man from Kansas City, had recently become a Christian, and knew that the same Jesus who had turned his life around could do it for his Muslim friend, too. But Tass would somehow have to overcome his prejudice against Jews as, of course, Jesus is Jewish.

Tass found that hard to take, but he did nevertheless submit to Christ in a dramatic conversion experience in which he heard the words "I am the way, the truth and the life" coming from a burst of light surrounding him![3] He didn't realize they were the same words spoken by Jesus during the Last Supper.

He was radically changed and family life was dramatically restored as his wife and two children also became disciples of the Jewish Messiah. Sadly, however, his parents and siblings cut him off, and on a visit home he narrowly escaped an "honor killing" for having disgraced the family by turning away from Islam when it seemed his older brother was somehow prevented by an unseen hand from reaching

---

2 Tass Saada with Dean Merrill, *Once an Arafat Man*, Tyndale Publishing, p. 103.

3 Saada, ibid, p. 105.

for the revolver so obviously bulging from his tunic;[4] there has been much reconciliation among them since.

Tass began to speak of his experience at churches, mosques, and synagogues all over America, eventually believing God was calling him back to the Middle East to promote the message of reconciliation through Jesus.

He started a kindergarten in Gaza to bring hope to Arab children and families caught up in the crossfire amid the poverty and rubble, but when Hamas took control in 2007 he was forced to withdraw and re-locate to Jericho in the West Bank, where he is now running a project called Hope for Ishmael, dedicated to reconciliation between Jews and Arabs.

Amazingly, the property he bought for this purpose is situated right opposite the village on the east bank of the Jordan where he shot and killed Israeli soldiers back in 1968.

"This was the place where so long ago I had come to fight and take life," he records in his book *Once an Arafat Man*. "Now God was bringing me back to do good and give life!"[5]

He had initially struggled to forgive himself for the brutality of snuffing out the lives of people God had created, but in time he fully grasped the depth of Christ's amazing grace. He realized, on reading the Bible, that there was actually more about Ishmael (Abraham's son by his servant Hagar) in the Jewish Scriptures than in the Qu'ran, and that God intends to bless Ishmael's descendants as well as those of Isaac (the son promised to Abraham and Sarah).

Shortly before Yasser Arafat died, Tass was given the chance of sharing his testimony with the PLO boss and challenging him to make his own peace with God. A colleague is

---

4 Saada, ibid, pp. 172-173.
5 Saada, ibid, p. 192.

said to have later gone even further by leading Arafat in the sinner's prayer—seeking forgiveness and new life from Jesus.

Writing of the Israeli-Palestinian conflict, Tass says, "I am convinced, from my reading of Scripture, that God wants the Jews to be living in this land. He promised it to them long ago through his prophets, and he has never changed his mind on that. So to try to throw them out is to fight against God. That is why we Arabs, in spite of our larger numbers, our petrodollars, and all the rest, have never been able to defeat Israel."

God loves both Arabs and Jews, neither of whom has lived up to their divine destiny, he writes, and there *is* a place for the "alien" in the Holy Land, according to the prophet Ezekiel (47:21-23). Jews and "foreigners" were meant to enjoy it together.

On the repeated failures of politicians to strike a peace accord, Tass is convinced that only Jesus can ultimately break down barriers—though he squarely faces up to the duplicitous nature of Arab dealings, an example of which was Arafat's statement of intent at the 1993 Oslo talks for which he (along with Yitzhak Rabin and Shimon Peres) was awarded the Nobel Peace Prize. This was for promising that the PLO charter would be changed to remove all calls for the destruction of Israel. But it never happened! The charter was never changed.

Tass comments, "There is a cultural problem here, in that lying is viewed within Islam as an acceptable tactic if it advances the goals of the religion."[6]

But he is also scathing of certain churches who invite him to talk about reconciliation in the Middle East, but are themselves not reconciled with the church down the road!

6   Saada, ibid, p. 197.

Tass also runs a humanitarian work for children, *Seeds of Hope*, whereas in the past he would have trained them to use a machine gun! And during the 2012 *At the Crossroads* conference he insisted that "Israel belongs to the Jewish people; it's in the Bible. So get over it!'"

But he also challenged Messianic Jews to seek justice for everyone.

"With man this is impossible, but with God all things are possible" (Matthew 19:26).

Another former Muslim, who addressed the inaugural conference two years earlier, told how he grew up hating the Jews but now loves them. Unnamed for his own protection, he was beaten and burned with cigarettes by his own family after deciding to follow Jesus, but his uncle fell down dead the day he threatened to kill him! His entire family subsequently became believers. And yet he still saw the Jews as enemies until he attended a conference in Jordan where two Jewish believers were talking about the work in Israel.

"I stood up and yelled, 'Who are you? You stole our land!' But the Lord stopped me, saying, 'What are you talking about? It's My land.'

"This is a big testimony—Jews and Arabs together in the Kingdom of God!" he told the Christ Church audience. "It's amazing to be here among my brothers and sisters," he added. "Only Jesus can give us love for one another."

Sons of Abraham Reconciled

So as politicians lick their wounds over yet another failure to strike a deal between Israelis and Palestinians, Jewish and Arab pastors have demonstrated how it is done.

Deeply moving gestures of peace between representatives of nations perceived as enemies of one another were made throughout the four-day gathering held on the theme of "fostering a reunion of the sons of Abraham."

At the final session on the Friday evening, Israeli and Turkish pastors prayed for their brothers from Egypt who were experiencing great upheaval with three regimes in as many years and the Christians facing a fiery trial. And yet the church there is experiencing unprecedented unity with even Coptics and evangelicals sharing communion together. "It's incredible what persecution can do," said a conference spokesman.

Among the delegates was a pilot with Egypt's national airline, who flies over this "highway," and who said he was brought up to see Israel as an enemy. But God has spoken to him about that and he has repented of his attitude. "God said to me, 'I love these people.' And as a woman from Cyprus said earlier in this conference, how can you hate the Jewish people when they gave us Jesus?" He added, "It's a real honor to be among you people. You were called to be a blessing to the nations, and indeed you are."

And when he said how they needed prayer for their nation, many Israeli pastors came forward to lay hands on their brothers and send them home with their blessing. An Egyptian pastor then prayed for the Israelis, saying, "We proclaim we are brothers and sisters and one family in the name of Jesus."

Some of the delegates, many seeing Israel for the first time, had also been taken on tours between sessions, following the footsteps of Jesus around the shores of Galilee and other significant Holy Land sites, as well as witnessing the horrors of Jewish suffering on a visit to the Yad Vashem Holocaust Museum.

Again, the corporate worship with songs of praise in five languages created a sense of God's presence that was tangible. A young Iranian woman led worship for a time on the keyboard, singing passionately about Jesus in Farsi, her native language, as she grieved for friends in prison for their faith. She said she had many friends from school and university days who testified of visions and dreams of Jesus, but had succumbed to fear of the consequences of changing their religion because some have been sentenced to death for this.

At the end of the conference, Ali prayed for Israel (in Turkish, translated through headsets for those who needed them): "Send your Spirit upon this country. That's the reason we've come. Right now we ask for blessing on the people of Israel."

Christ Church rector David Pileggi, in his closing remarks, said he trusts that the event will help present a clearer picture of what God is doing in the Middle East, so often blurred by a constant focus on conflict.

"The aim had always been to strengthen the developing network of mutual co-operation and explore more practically how all the sons of Abraham can together help build a 'highway' of blessing in the region."

And he reiterated the vision of Christ Church that the "church and compound would actually be a refuge for the people of Israel and a place where the nations find healing."

The conference was rounded off by Avner Boskey, an Israeli pastor from Beersheva, who said that what satan had meant for evil (in terms of the conflict between the sons of

Abraham), God was working out for good, just as he had done with the patriarch Joseph whose brothers had thrown him down a well. He ended up as second-in-charge of all Egypt, and was able to rescue his brothers from famine and death.

I should say that while this conference was truly unique in that Arabs from countries effectively at war with Israel were to be seen embracing their Jewish brothers in Jerusalem, I am aware that reconciliation work between Arab and Jew has been going on for some time within Israel itself. The fact is that they worship together in congregations throughout the land and, as I mentioned earlier, I witnessed this myself at Mt. Carmel in David and Karen Davis' congregation.

After spending much of the weekend writing up further reports and meeting deadlines, Monday—my last full day in Jerusalem—was more relaxing and I was able to gently wind down while also tying up some loose ends, though I had still not actually finished sending stories out, partly because I was deliberately trying to stagger what would have been a relent-less bombardment of copy falling on certain news-desks, and also because I was waiting for some photos from Carino.

So I decided to take a huge circular walk around the city, fulfilling various tasks on the way. At last I was able to catch up with Remi Rauh, our Swiss-German friend from Ireland days who runs a mission selling Arabic Christian literature. Because he was in between tasks and had his gorgeous two little boys strapped fast asleep in the back of his car, I caught a lift with him and he drove me down to Christ Church. It had been a dozen or so years since we had last seen each other. We used to work together with the children during the summer conferences at the Christian Renewal Center in

County Down. He is married to Laura, an American, whose parents are running a church on the Mount of Olives.

I had another tasty lunch at Christ Church followed by coffee and, for the first time on my trip, picked up a copy of the *Jerusalem Post*, an absorbing read. What mostly caught my attention was a report of a riot that had taken place at the Damascus Gate which I had somehow missed despite passing that way at least twice a day. A group of Palestinians were throwing rocks at police and burning the Israeli flag in "celebration" of what in their language is known as Catastrophe Day—the day in 1948 when modern Israel was born.[7]

I also had a chat during lunch with Aaron Eime, a 43-year-old Australian who is in charge of the Heritage Center and apparently also an excellent teacher, though I only ever saw him in action taking services and giving short words—very competently I might add.

After lunch, I resumed my walk, following my favorite running route at a slower pace, which allowed me to savor the sights, sounds, and smells all the more deeply, and also take some photos of scenes I had only viewed "on the run" such as that of the Mount of Olives from the "Peace Forest" promenade along with the iconic olive trees in the foreground. Of course, the bright sunshine made viewing of the subject quite a challenge, but I usually found a bit of shade to help me see what I was photographing.

I then headed for Ben Yehuda Street, where I had located a flower shop the day before, because I wanted to buy a pot

---

7 They commemorate this the day after Israel's Gregorian calendar Independence Day, which is May 14. The Israelis celebrate it according to the Hebrew calendar which falls on different Gregorian dates each year. In 2014 it was May 5-6.; in 2015, April 22-23.

plant for Caroline. Until then, I hadn't seen a flower shop all fortnight, and started to wonder if they existed in Israel, so naturally I prayed and within minutes there it was! Wine (for Don) wasn't so difficult to find. Arriving back at the flat somewhat more heavily laden, I booked a sharoot (airport shuttle bus/taxi) to pick me up at 12:45 the following day, which would give me plenty of time for my 5:15 p.m. flight home. Ahem!

11

Open Mike in Jerusalem

Before flying off, I managed to pen these personal reflections of what had been an intense but amazing fortnight in the city of the Great King, writing along the themes of reconciliation, running, and praising God in a crowded Jewish bar.[1]

The idea of a conference in Jerusalem aimed at fostering deeper bonds between Arab Christians and Jewish followers of Jesus had inspired me from the moment I heard of it.

And now that the delegates to *At the Crossroads* are making their way back home at various points of the Middle East compass, I can report without fear of exaggeration that, in 40 years of journalism and a little more as a Christian, what I have witnessed was beyond my wildest dreams.

As the Scripture says, "No eye has seen, nor ear has heard, nor mind has conceived what God has prepared for those who love him."

The invitation-only gathering involved some 100 pastors from many of the nations perceived as enemies of Israel coming to sample the hospitality of their Jewish brothers at Christ Church.

---

1 The rest of this section is an edited version of a previously published article: "Open Mic Night in Jerusalem," *Gateway News*, South Africa, May 22 2014.

As if being in this glorious ancient city—described by the psalmist 3,000 years ago as "beautiful for situation, the joy of the whole earth"—wasn't enough, the conference venue too (a tranquil oasis of peace just inside the walls of the Old City) was something of a microcosm of all that is best about this magnificent place set on Mount Zion, some 3,000 ft. above-sea-level.

As a runner, I was able to sample the city in all its splendor via a few rather hot and hilly running excursions, including the six-mile round trip to the top of the Hebron Road and up onto the newly-constructed "Peace Forest" promenade—running alongside the pre-1967 border—affording stunning views of the Mount of Olives where Jesus, the Prince of Peace, is set to return any time soon.

Yes, it is paradoxical—throbbing with life and festive noise as its 800,000 population seem permanently to be partying, its streets peacefully lined with palms and flowering trees and its splendid stone buildings silently gleaming in the sun. At the same time it's the immovable rock to which the prophet Zechariah referred, fought over for millennia in an ultimately futile bid to rob Israel of her prized possession, the city God calls his own.

So we have tension here requiring young soldiers to patrol the streets with menacing weapons and, for those of us who follow the Man who died in this city for the sins of all, there is an awareness of a spiritual battle going on for the souls of its inhabitants because, after all, the message of Jesus was "for the Jew first" (Romans 1:16).

In this respect I had the great pleasure and privilege of talking to a number of its residents, especially at Mike's Place, a friendly bar on Jaffa Road where I dropped in a few times on my way home to the apartment where my delightful Australian hosts looked after me with such extraordinary kindness.

On my first visit to Mike's Place, I engaged in deep conversations about faith with three young Jewish men and was then invited by a man behind the bar to their weekly "open mic" session the following evening in the cellar below, where live music is played every night. My guitar was back in England, but he said I could borrow his. So I came along for the show late the following night, only one day before the *Crossroads* event, and joined a lively crowd of young people out having a good time. Having prayed about it, I got the feeling it was part of the "open door" the Lord had promised me before I left.

Sitting at the bar waiting my turn with Ooi Peng Ee, a charming businessman from Singapore, I have to confess I was beginning to get nervous, worrying that I might forget the words and perhaps even the chord sequences. I can't imagine what those X-factor contestants must go through. While I help to lead worship at my home church in North Nottinghamshire, I have never done anything like this before, though I do regularly perform at family parties. I was third up on stage, but once I was under the spotlight, a huge calm descended on me and I just knew I was in the place God wanted me to be.

So having hoisted the borrowed guitar over my shoulders, I launched out with the Elvis song, "Can't Help Falling in Love," having dedicated it to my wife Linda back home in England and told them how much I loved Jerusalem, and

knew after just a few bars that I had hit the right
note with my twenty-something audience who
were clearly entering into the spirit of this fabu-
lously romantic song. The headache I had been
nursing all day suddenly disappeared as I simply
relaxed and enjoyed myself.

As the cheers died down, I followed it with
"You Raise Me Up," having explained that
it said something about my faith. Indeed it is
effectively a worship song despite not actually
mentioning God by name and proved the key to
unlocking the door of at least one young Jewish
man there that night.[2]

As I returned to my seat to cries of "awesome" from various customers, Moshe (the
young man) put his arms around me, saying
how much he had enjoyed it, and I talked with
him about Jesus for the next half-hour. He had
many questions....

He certainly had issues over many points, and it was
hard conducting the conversation against the background of
so much noise (music and general chat). "If He was the Son
of God," he asked, "why did He have to come down and live
among us?" This obviously led me to explain why He had
to die. Moshe even understood the Trinity as a result of my
simple illustration of ice, water, and steam all being compo-
nents of the same matter.

But his eyes lit up when I explained how
Jesus (Yeshua) was the ultimate Passover Lamb.
He seemed to understand.

And as I urged him to place the blood of
Jesus (metaphorically speaking) on his heart
just as his ancestors had done on the doorposts

---

2 "You Raise Me Up," music by Secret Garden's Rolf Lovland,
lyrics by Brendan Graham, sung by many well-known artists,
including the Celtic Women.

of their houses the night they were freed from slavery in Egypt, he seemed almost ready to take a step towards a life of total fulfillment only possible through the Messiah.

All of which—both this experience and the privilege of reporting on the conference—fulfilled a word spoken into my life so many times: "How beautiful on the mountains are the feet of those who bring good news, who proclaim peace, who bring good tidings, who proclaim salvation, who say to Zion, 'Your God reigns!'" (Isaiah 52:7).[3]

Airport Staff on Strike!

With the clock approaching midnight, I made my excuses (the conference was starting the next day) and left before my slippers turned to glass, but I was walking on air! What's more, my performance had been recorded for posterity and can be viewed on YouTube, thanks to my new friend from Singapore, Ooi Peng Ee. A business executive working in publishing, his daughter had come across a very popular "open mic" culture while at Durham University in England and subsequently introduced it to Singapore. So he has followed her special interest, and duly videoed my act.

Tuesday, May 20, finally arrived, and I packed my cases for the flight home. It was my spiritual birthday—the 42nd anniversary of inviting Jesus into my life—and I was ready for a nice-n-easy trip back into the loving arms of Linda! I hoped! But the tension wasn't over yet. I took a stroll down to Christ Church to say goodbye to friends, only to be met by a panicking receptionist aware that I was flying out that day,

---

3 The author in "Open Mic Night in Jerusalem," *Gateway News*, South Africa, May 22 2014.

telling me, "You'd better get yourself to the airport quick! They're on strike, and if you don't go now you'll miss your flight!"

Well, I'd booked my sharoot, and it was going to be far too complicated for me to change all that. So I figured I'd stick to Plan A and trust the Lord—and send another urgent text to Linda! This time I *was* coming home, strike permitting! It wasn't the pilots refusing to fly, but the ground staff who were working-to-rule, as it turned out, but the effect was potentially as disabling with long queues forecast. Nevertheless, I was determined to remain calm; as I'd been telling myself throughout my stay, Jesus never went about in a mad hurry—and he got a lot done in just three years!

The sharoot duly picked me up bang on time. It is a very efficient and relatively inexpensive mode of transport. They drop you off or pick you up as close as they can to where you are and want to go. But we then seemed to whizz around the city in endless circles trying to locate other passengers, who at one stop failed to turn up. When finally we seemed well on our way down the highway towards Tel Aviv I came in for another shock. A tweet from my phone indicated I had received a text, and it was from Linda to say the effects of the strike were far worse than at first thought. In her typically efficient way, she had been checking out the situation on the internet, and the state of play was that all El Al flights scheduled for take-off from Tel Aviv before 9 p.m. had been cancelled. So there was still a chance of me being at the heart of an "international incident" after all. I contemplated sleeping at Ben Gurion Airport and missing my train connection at King's Cross, London, the following afternoon. I had planned to stay overnight with my mum in north London. She would be very disappointed if I missed seeing her, and missing the train would prove costly as my cheap advanced ticket only applied to the 14:25 departure. Surely, things could only get better!

I was dropped off at the airport with at least the customary three hours to spare that they require these days. Then I got the message that everything was back on schedule, only I was greeted by a seething mass of humanity as I entered the main concourse and couldn't for the life of me distinguish one queue from another. I hadn't the foggiest clue which line I was meant to be joining. And it was getting hotter by the minute (Tel Aviv is a lot warmer than Jerusalem anyway) as I wearily dragged my bags while inching forward at a snail's pace. Eventually I got to the head of the queue, only to be asked by the customs officer if I had any DVDs, at which point I swung around to apologize to those behind me. DVDs are a particular security risk, and Don had put three in my bag with the very best of motives. One of them was entitled *Murder at 50,000 ft.*, a movie made long before airborne terrorism became a global security issue. Perhaps this is where those 9/11 "pilots" got their ideas?

Finally, in the departure lounge, I ordered a pint of well-earned Israeli beer at the bar, only to be told they only had half-pint glasses, which amounted to extra expense apart from anything else. Two halves don't make a whole. I know that's what they taught you at school, but two halves at 23 shekels each make 46, whereas a pint at 28 shekels makes— you guessed it, 28!

Anyway, who was I to complain when I learned that, after all, the plane was boarding on time? However, due to the baggage-handler "go-slow," there *was* an hour delay before take-off, which meant that we were sitting in our seats, strapped in and ready to go, for 90 minutes. In the end I arrived at mum's at midnight, and it was very good of her to wait up for me. My son, Julian, a garden designer and journalist who had just attended the Chelsea Flower Show press day, had left a few Budweisers in the fridge for me, which I downed in no time. I hadn't had a drop to drink since dinner was served around 8 p.m.

After spending a lovely morning catching up with Mum, I set off for King's Cross and arrived there with an hour or more to spare. So I sat down and relaxed with a coffee, mysteriously given to me "on the house," which I took to be an extra blessing from the Lord! And I got talking at great depth with an Oxford professor (of electronics)—about politics, the history of CMJ, the place of the Jews in God's great plan, and why Jesus had come for them first! Quite extraordinary! His eyes lit up, and I gave him my card before catching the *Flying Scotsman* home for a wonderful reunion with my gorgeous, darling wife!

But would you believe it? I had barely walked through the front door when I received an urgent call from Jane Moxon, CMJ's UK development officer, asking me if I would stand in for Owen Hoskin, who was on a tour of the Lake District speaking about our work, but had been recalled to Israel to give evidence in a court case relating to residency permits, as I recall. It was Wednesday evening, and I had just arrived home exhausted from a hugely intense trip to Israel. "Could I speak in Carlisle on Saturday? It's just over the Pennines." Actually, it's just one stop short of Scotland, and it was quite impracticable as I had a BBC interview early on Sunday morning.

In the end, we had to rouse ourselves at 5:30 a.m. (neither of us are morning people) for the live interview with BBC Radio Sheffield some 30 miles away. It went well enough,

I think, but you would have to ask listeners to really know. According to Linda, I gave both politicians and the media a lot of stick, so may not have been winning friends with my hosts. But the presenter, who handled it very professionally, was obviously challenged by one of my online reports, which he had read. He suggested that if politicians had been at the conference, they would have learned some useful stuff!

Yes, I believe our BBC man hit the nail on the head. Politicians could well have benefited from being at a conference where participants engaged not only in talk, but also in acting out the perfect "deal" Jesus had won for us by reconciling us through His death on the cross.

They might also have learned that a right understanding of history, of Israel, of the God of the Bible, and of truth itself is necessary before we can fully and adequately grasp what is happening on today's fast-changing world scene.

Which is why, in the following chapters, I intend to tackle some of these major issues, many of which have gotten our men of influence in a terrible muddle in recent decades— especially since the Judeo-Christian foundations of Western civilization have begun to crumble before our eyes.

12

Israel Accused of Apartheid!

As a proud South African, in spite of over 40 years living in Britain, I am ashamed to say that my government has opted for a progressive disengagement with Israel. And presumably in the light of this and a general increase of anti-Semitism there, Jews in South Africa have been warned (by Israeli officials) to begin emigrating. International Relations Minister Maite Nkoana-Mashabane has evidently fallen for the Palestinian/Arab propaganda which has every left-leaning politician and media outlet accusing the Jewish state of practicing apartheid.

This is a travesty of the truth that has been fomented and given "Christian" credibility by none other than anti-apartheid legend Desmond Tutu, the Nobel Prize-winning former Archbishop of Cape Town, who should have known better. Atheist practitioners can perhaps be expected to swallow such undiluted drivel, but Bible-believing Christians, who should weigh everything in the light of Scripture, have no excuse.

True, a wall has been built to keep potential suicide bombers from launching their murderous raids from the Palestinian territories. And it has worked! But this can hardly be compared with the separate development policy of Afrikaner-led South Africa, which restricted black citizens to certain areas and denied them political and other rights including access to "whites-only" jobs.

The apartheid accusation is ludicrous. I lived through the apartheid era in South Africa, and to make such a comparison is patently absurd. The minority Arab citizens in Israel have the same rights as their fellow Jewish citizens, which was never the case in my country between 1948 and the early 1990's when black people had to live in their own designated areas. In Israel, Arabs are even represented in the Knesset (Parliament)—in fact, I have recently met a Muslim Arab Israeli diplomat! In South Africa, blacks had no vote, their pay was much lower than that of white people doing the same job, and access to education was limited. And who was it that led the way in the old white Parliament for blacks to be given equal rights, but a wonderful, feisty Jewish lady called Mrs. Helen Suzman?

How can an apartheid state have Jews and Arabs working together in government and side by side in hospitals? There are 1.6 million Arabs living in Israel—that's twenty percent of the population. And yet Mahmoud Abbas will not allow any Jews to live in his proposed state of "Palestine." So who's practicing apartheid?

Worse still, the new Hamas textbooks in Gaza teach that "all of Palestine from the Mediterranean Sea to the River Jordan belongs to us—to us Muslims." So no room for Jews anywhere in the region then! Just remember this, South Africa. You may forsake Israel, but God will never do so (Jeremiah 31:35-37).

What an irony, too, that the new South African government chooses to condemn Israel as an apartheid state when it was the Jewish community among the ruling white population who were at the forefront of the battle against apartheid in South Africa. According to International Christian Embassy Jerusalem director Luba Mayekiso, sixty percent of the Treason Trial accused were Jewish, and all those classified white at the Rivonia Trial were Jews. These were the notorious trials at which Nelson Mandela and his colleagues paid dearly for their struggle against apartheid. Then there was the indefatigable Mrs. Suzman who, for decades in the old white Parliament when blacks had no voice, campaigned on their behalf for their political rights.

Financing the Progressive Party, which Helen represented as its lone MP (Member of Parliament) for many years, was Harry Oppenheimer, a Jewish businessman who embraced Christianity on his marriage to Bridget McCall. However, he continued supporting Jewish causes and, as boss of the Anglo-American and De Beers mining conglomerates, made a significant contribution to Israel's economy by ensuring that his diamonds were sent to the state which became a world leader in polishing and cutting the precious stones. He personally financed the launch of the specifically anti-apartheid Progressive Party in 1959 (my mother drove 1,000 miles to Cape Town in a 500cc Fiat to attend the launch and I was a "young delegate" at their 1969 conference). Mrs. Suzman singlehandedly took on the might of South Africa's Nationalist government for many years before the apartheid structure started to crumble. I believe she was used as one of the "bouncing bombs" that eventually cracked the system, just as in the famous Dambusters' raid on the great German dams during World War II.

So it's "Thank you very much for your support; now we're going to kick you!"

Frankly, it stinks, and is nothing less than rank anti-Semitism ignited by gross ignorance, prejudice, and skewed intelligence. In fact, it is tantamount to the new black-led regime threatening to shoot itself in the foot. Not much of a legacy for Nelson Mandela, for whom I have the greatest respect.

It would be an understatement to say that the Jews of South Africa have contributed hugely to the strength of its economy over the years. So to set a process in motion whereby you stand to lose some of your best brains—people who have helped build up the country with their wealth, inventiveness, ingenuity, and remarkable skills—is suicidal in the extreme and has dark overtones of the Nazi era in pre-war Germany.

As one who is proud to have attended St. Andrew's College—one of South Africa's top private schools—I am starting to wonder if the government there is re-writing the history taught in its state schools, just as the Palestinian Arabs have done in the Middle East where they deny that Israel ever had a claim to the land.

However, my hope and prayer is that sense and wisdom will in the end prevail. Twenty years ago South Africa became a model for the rest of the world with the reconciliation process (triggered by Desmond Tutu to his great credit) that followed the relatively peaceful transfer of power from white minority to black majority rule.

But that process—and this is so important to grasp—was firmly grounded in the country's deep Christian roots. And unless this is recaptured, South Africa's future is bleak indeed. Nelson Mandela himself was well-read in Afrikaans literature and understood their Biblical faith. And because he grew up among, and was educated by, Methodist missionaries, he knew about the essential role of forgiveness.

But where is the truth and reconciliation now? Should we not try to preside over such a process in the Middle East too by embracing Israel as well as Arabs, rather than favoring one over the other on the questionable pretext of apartheid while ignoring the atrocities committed against Israelis by Hamas-led Palestinian extremists, not to mention the corruption of its leaders?

Ultimate reconciliation, even in the Middle East, is to be found in the cross of Jesus Christ, through whom forgiveness of our shared sin is procured for Jew and Gentile, black and white, Catholic and Protestant, Arab and Israeli. In Christ all are able to experience brotherly love as one happy family. For Jesus took all our sins (however heinous) upon Himself so that we might have access to God without hindrance, and learn to forgive one another!

Meanwhile, in Ireland, where considerable progress has been made towards reconciliation between Catholic and Protestant communities, yellow stickers, reading *"For justice in Palestine, boycott Israel,"* have been discovered on Israeli products. The labels have evidently been placed by the Boycott, Divestment and Sanctions (BDS) campaign on many items including a pack of dates from the Jordan Valley.

And, more shocking still, it is reported that similar stickers have been placed on other products in the Tesco supermarket chain, originally established by Jewish businessman Jack Cohen, the son of Jewish immigrants from Poland whose grandchildren and great-grandchildren now live in Israel.

Sources in Israel's Foreign Ministry said it was not by chance that the BDS organization chose to express its protest with a yellow sticker, which is reminiscent of the dark days of anti-Semitism in Nazi Germany.

Responding to my protest, Tesco customer service spokesman Adam Hale said, "I am sorry to learn that you are unhappy with the placement of yellow stickers on products from Israel. I can confirm that it is not our practice for these stickers to be placed on our products and we understand that these have been placed on our products by a campaign group called BDS, not by our in-store colleagues or suppliers."

Arab Shepherd Boy Becomes Israeli Diplomat

The story of a Bedouin shepherd boy turned Israeli diplomat comes as a slap in the face for those accusing the Jewish state of practicing apartheid. For Ishmael Khaldi, who grew up living in tents in the hills of Western Galilee, defies the stereotypes created by the media of Arabs perpetually in conflict with their Semitic brothers. He shared his thoughts at a conference I attended in York in 2013 that was sponsored by The Emmaus Group, an organization that speaks out against the mistreatment of Christians and Jews in Muslim regions. [1]

Representing his country in some very hostile environments—including being a government spokesman during Israel's 2005 pull-out from the Gaza Strip—Ishmael has often been misunderstood and derided by fellow Arabs, some of whom see him as a traitor to the cause of Palestinian aspirations. But he had grown up loving the Jewish people, who

---

1   A conference in York, UK, by the Emmaus Group, http:// emmaus-group.org Nov. 16, 2013.

befriended and helped Bedouin families like his in the early stages of Israel's development when kibbutz farmers provided employment and shared their facilities.

Even during his years spent as Israel's deputy consul general to the U.S. Pacific Northwest in San Francisco, he was shocked by the amount of anti-Israel sentiment he encountered, particularly on the university campuses. Many struggled to get their heads around how a Muslim Arab could represent the aspirations of the Jewish state.

Fluent in Hebrew, Ishmael has also come under fire from left-wing students in the UK who shouted so loudly when he addressed the University of Edinburgh in Scotland in 2011 that he was unable to speak (so much for freedom of speech).[2] In spite of his treatment there, he is determined to keep on defending the country in which he has also served as a policeman.

Recognizing that Israel is far from perfect, he is nevertheless proud to serve the only democracy in the Middle East where minorities are generally treated fairly. And as if the political tightrope hasn't been tricky enough for him to negotiate, he has also had to make the huge leap from the simple nomadic lifestyle he once led to that of an influential government official in a high-tech modern world.

Nowhere was this contrast greater than when, on his first trip to America as a young man, he took a shortcut to the opposite platform of the New York subway by stepping over the tracks, naively unaware of the danger of being electrocuted. When he was about to try it a second time days later, his new Israeli friend stopped him, explaining the risk.

---

2 "The silencing of Ishmael Khaldi," YouTube video, Feb 7, 2011
https://www.youtube.com/watch?v=k7ZznKXpwnM

On the question of apartheid in Israel, he is emphatic, "Jews and Arabs use the same buses, clinics, government offices, universities, theaters, restaurants, soccer fields, and beaches."

Obviously fully conversant with what apartheid was really like for blacks in white-led South Africa, he adds, "All Israeli citizens, regardless of religion or ethnic origins, are equal before the law, the same law that accords full political, civil, and human rights to its entire population, including its more than one million Arab citizens, some of whom serve in the Israeli parliament. Israel is the only country in the world to have sought out and brought to its shores, entirely on its own initiative, tens of thousands of black Africans for purposes other than slavery, granting them full citizenship."[3]

Ishmael's full story is told in *A Shepherd's Journey: The story of Israel's first Bedouin diplomat*, which he published himself.

No Safe Haven for Palestinian Christian

Meanwhile, a young Palestinian woman who has been granted asylum in Britain after receiving death threats for taking a stand against corruption among her own people has received further such threats since arriving in the UK.

Christy Anastas, an Arab Christian from Bethlehem, has spoken of her plight on YouTube,[4] but I also heard her speak at the Emmaus Group conference in York just mentioned.[5] She says Christians have been driven out of Palestinian areas by the intimidation of Islamic fundamentalists. Her own hometown, the birthplace of Jesus, which had

---

3 Ishmael Khaldi, *A Shepherd's Journey: The story of Israel's first Bedouin diplomat,* Ishmael Khaldi, 2010, pp. 117-118.

4 https://www.youtube.com/watch?v=XyQZcKXeI4U

5 Emmaus Group conference, York, UK, Nov. 16, 2013.

a majority Christian population until quite recently, is now almost totally taken over by Muslims.

She believes the Israeli authorities were right to build the security wall that has led to so much worldwide controversy "because it has stopped my people from blowing themselves up," referring to the suicide bombers who have brought such terror to the streets of Jerusalem and beyond.

Christy accuses the Palestinian Authority of corruption and says its people would be "rich" if the aid money poured in from the outside world was used for the benefit of all its citizens. In fact, Palestinians are killing each other, as happened between the Hamas and Fatah parties in 2006.

Women in the Palestinian territories have no rights and are treated as mere possessions, not human beings. There has also been an exponential rise in "honor killings" in which individuals who have allegedly brought shame on their families have been summarily executed without recourse to the rule of law.

Christy became convinced that God has an everlasting covenant with the Jews after learning how they miraculously overcame armies much greater than their own in the Yom Kippur War of 1973 despite having to fight on more than one front. She further asks why, if Muslims and Christians predominate in so many nations of the world, the Jewish people can't be allowed to have just one country they can call their own.

Christy testified that she was sexually harassed on a constant basis during her student days, but it wasn't until after speaking out and receiving death threats that she felt forced to leave her homeland and seek asylum in Britain. It clearly hasn't proved to be the safe haven for which she was hoping, however. "I have received death threats in the UK, too," she said.

The truth is that Christy is exposing one of the biggest lies around—that the poor Palestinians are squirming helplessly under Israel's bullying jackboot—whereas the reality is very different. It's an upside-down world we live in.

Someone has tweeted that, though liberal media like *The Guardian* are quick to rally to the Palestinian cause, it doesn't seem to occur to them that they are taking sides with what a recent survey has discovered to be an extremely homophobic society.[6] But as Israel's great prophet Isaiah wrote some 2,700 years ago: "Woe to those who call evil good and good evil, who put darkness for light and light for darkness, who put bitter for sweet and sweet for bitter" (Isaiah 5:20).

I pray that the bitterness of evil and corruption that has hounded Christy out of her homeland will turn sweet in the coming days as she tastes the goodness of her Lord and Savior Jesus, the Jewish Messiah.

---

6 "The Global Divide on Homosexuality," PewResearchCenter, June 4, 2013, http://www.pewglobal.org/2013/06/04/the-global-divide-on-homosexuality/

13

Boycott Israel Protest Flawed

Supporters of the Jewish state have come up with a BIG idea! Recent campaigns to Boycott Israeli Goods have been turned on their head by shoppers who have chosen to use the same acronym (BIG) for their own protest.

Supporters of Buy Israeli Goods are hoping to pre-empt a renewed effort to isolate the Jewish nation by rightly drawing the attention of major supermarkets to the flaws of an argument that goes something like this: Israel is an apartheid state that bullies its Palestinian neighbors and we should have no more to do with her.

It's a line of thinking that basically reflects what both the Arab and Western media generally portray, but comes nowhere near a true understanding of the situation.

The fact is that Israel is the only true democracy in the entire Middle East, where "enemy" states are collapsing from within as rival groups fight each other. Israelis desire peace with their neighbors, but were forced to erect a protecting wall to prevent suicide bombers from doing their worst. Yet this hasn't stopped rockets from being fired from Gaza on an almost continual basis. If your town was rained upon by rockets in this way, would you just shrug it off, or would you not expect your Government to do everything in their power to protect you? So why do you ignore attacks on the Jews while choosing to concentrate on the alleged injustice they are inflicting on Arabs?

I very much doubt if the boycott advocates would go all the way in their efforts if they really knew the extent of the merchandise produced by little old Israel, or by Jewish people in other lands. It would mean a change of lifestyle few would be prepared to endure.

We are not just talking about oranges, sharon fruit, wine, and a few other products we could easily leave out of our shopping baskets without upsetting our appetites too much. Are they prepared to sacrifice their mobile phones, computers, and so many other trappings of modern life for the cause? It is no secret that Israel has long been an international hub in the development and production of modern technology from which we all now benefit and without which much of our commerce would grind to a shuddering halt.

For example, you would have to stop googling for all that vital information as Google founders Larry Page and Sergey Brin are both Jews. You would have to close down your Facebook account because 29-year-old Jewish-American Mark Zuckerberg founded the facility. You would have to stop watching Steven Spielberg movies and chuck out all your Bob Dylan and Barbra Streisand albums. And, to top it all, you would need to close down your computers as Microsoft boss Steve Ballmer and Dell Computers founder and CEO Michael Dell are both Jewish.

The latest news is that internet search engine giant Google has purchased the Israeli navigation software maker Waze for over a billion dollars. Waze's smartphone application combines GPS navigation software with social networking features, enabling users to adapt to changing road conditions, such as speed traps and accidents, in real time.

For the record, a Sainsbury's[1] spokeswoman said in a statement answering my own concerns over the boycott campaign:

> "We want to offer our customers the best quality products throughout the year. In the past we have received requests to boycott the products of various countries and suppliers. However, as a non-political organization, we source our products according to their ability to meet our quality, safety, and ethical standards.
>
> "We prefer to give our customers the opportunity to make their own decision in terms of the products they buy. That is why we work hard to label our products clearly and accurately so that our customers can make an informed choice when shopping. We are founding members of the Ethical Trading Initiative and require all our suppliers to meet the ETI Base Code for ethical sourcing which covers nine key principles including safe and hygienic working conditions and payment of a fair wage."

Co-op Pays Dearly for Israeli Boycott

Shortly after learning of the Co-operative Group's decision to back the Boycott Israeli Goods campaign, we discovered that they were in serious financial trouble. This isn't surprising since, as I have already pointed out, those who bless Israel will themselves be blessed while those who curse her will come under God's judgment (Genesis 12:3).

---

1 A major grocery store chain in the UK.

I realize that the Co-op was no doubt already in big trouble before "buying" the campaign ticket, but the timing of the financial announcement nevertheless provides an apt lesson in how not to conduct business.

The BIG boycott movement was borne out of grossly ill-informed propaganda of the worst sort, whose latest mantra is that Israel is an apartheid state. And yet, while leaders of the proposed Palestinian state have vowed that not a single Jew will be allowed to live in their territory, the Israeli Government has recently approved the allocation of 5,000 work permits for Palestinians from the West Bank, enabling them to work in Israel.

Israel has many faults—they are as secular a state as Britain despite their religious roots—but they are still special to God just as a father does not abandon his child because he has strayed from the principles on which he was nurtured. Yet isn't it extraordinary how so many today are focusing on the Israeli-Palestinian problem, in which their clear view is that the former are the bullies and the latter the victims, while all around the Jewish state the Middle East is in flames? And not content with that, Islamic fundamentalists are at the same time busy terrorizing Africa with bloodcurdling attacks on innocent civilians in Nigeria, Sudan, Kenya, and also Niger.

It was such a breath of fresh air to read Dominic Lawson's article in *The Independent*[2] in which he made this point with great clarity, mocking rock stars and others for being out of tune with reality and politicians for thinking that solving the Palestinian question is the key to Middle East peace. The Jews are always being blamed for trouble in the

---

2 Dominic Lawson, "So who still thinks Israel is the root of Middle East problems?" *The Independent,* Sept, 2, 2013.

world, but it would be ridiculous to blame them now for the conflicts in Syria and Egypt, Lawson wrote. Or indeed for the latest wave of terror in Iraq and Syria, I would add.

Now Israel's enemies are fighting each other, which puts one in mind of the occasion several millennia ago when a Moabite alliance set out to attack the Israelites, whom they greatly outnumbered. But the Jewish King Jehoshaphat put his trust in the Lord and led his people in worship as they went out to battle. Their enemies turned on each other and Israel triumphed.

I should say two things on this before moving on, however. First, though Egypt, Syria, and other surrounding states have indeed declared themselves enemies of Israel today, many of their people are peace-loving and I do not believe that Jews wish any evil upon them. On the contrary, whenever disasters occur around the world, Israel is often the first to offer help and expertise, and even now their hospitals are treating soldiers wounded across the border in Syria.

Secondly, Israel as a whole needs to restore their relationship with God, as they did in Jehoshaphat's day. They too have fallen into the ways of the world—with abortion and homosexuality rife, for example—and need to repent and return to the God of their fathers who is (or should be) at the center of their regular feasts.

Nevertheless, Syria, Iran, Hezbollah, or anyone else thinking of firing chemical weapons into Israel would be playing a very dangerous game. For Israeli Prime Minister Binyamin Netanyahu has vowed that while his country will not be the first to strike with their arsenal, they will certainly respond with force to any such attack. It is worth noting an, as yet, unfulfilled ancient prophecy about Damascus becoming "a heap of ruins" (Isaiah 17:1), a scenario which could well be the ghastly outcome of such an exchange.

It is now over 40 years since the 1973 Yom Kippur War when Israel was caught off guard celebrating their holiest day of the year (the Day of Atonement), but they have no intention of being caught napping again. Yet despite being unprepared and greatly outnumbered, they won that war—just as they had done in 1948 and 1967. In the Golan Heights during October 1973, 150 Israeli tanks faced 1,400 Syrian tanks and in the Suez region just 500 Israeli soldiers were up against 80,000 Egyptian soldiers while other Arab nations also contributed heavily to the cause.

Putting it crudely, the lessons of history would suggest that it's best not to mess with Israel even if, in your arrogance, you refuse to believe they are God's chosen people.

14

Tough-Talking Truth About Israel

The stark reality of Israel's vulnerability was brought into sharp focus when one of their leading politicians challenged British TV host Stephen Sackur with the question, "Would you hand over half of Britain to someone who keeps on killing you?"

Economy Minister Naftali Bennett, who entered politics after selling the software company he co-founded for $145 million, was being interviewed on February 25, 2014 for the BBC's HARDtalk current affairs program (on their World News and News Channel) and was being asked why he opposed sovereignty for the Palestinians.

"Every time Israel withdraws from land, they kill us…," he countered. "It's time to try a different approach." He wondered how many viewers realized how little land Israel's 8 million people actually have. "We only have one homeland. The Arabs have 22—300 times the size of our tiny state."

Ignorance of Israel's plight is further complicated due to the amount of propaganda eagerly swallowed by a gullible media hungry for anything that is perceived to tarnish the reputation of the Jewish state.

Prime Minister Binyamin Netanyahu's demand that the Palestinians recognize Israel's right to exist as a pre-condition for talks is surely perfectly reasonable because not to do so clearly signals an intention to continue the fight after winning their "half" of the deal—hardly a recipe for peace.

PLO spokeswoman Hanan Ashrawi was quoted in *The Independent* as saying that to recognize the Jewish state "would condone discrimination against members of Israel's Arab minority…."

What nauseating nonsense in light of the fact that Israel is the only democracy in the Middle East and includes Arabs in their Parliament, not to mention a Muslim Bedouin in their diplomatic corps.

As Bennett challenges, "Show me in Saudi Arabia a Jewish member of parliament; show me in Jordan; show me in Syria; show me in Lebanon… We're [also] the only democracy in the entire Middle East who really gives free rights and equal rights to women. Everyone can speak up in Israel and everyone does." As for apartheid, for which Israel stands accused, he says, "We've got apartheid going on in Lebanon. … In Syria they butchered 100,000 people. Why haven't sanctions been threatened on those states? We're not blowing up mosques like others are blowing up churches."

Ms. Ashrawi went on to say, "Israel was built on Palestinian land. We've been there for centuries. We are the victims of Zionism who were expelled and placed under occupation." And yet she has the gall to accuse Mr. Netanyahu of being disingenuous. The Palestinians never had a land; they are no more than an invention in terms of being a nation—a mixture of Arab people from surrounding lands.

Yes, the region was known as Palestine before the rebirth of Israel, but the Jews themselves were called Palestinians in those days and in that sense the PLO are guilty of identity theft! It was the Romans who renamed Israel Palestine in 136 AD as a final insult to the people whose land they ravaged because it stood for their ancient enemy the Philistines whose champion Goliath was slain at the hands of a young David. The truth is that Israel has been the ancestral homeland of the Jewish people for thousands of years and Jerusalem was their capital centuries before there was a London, Berlin, Paris, or Washington.

Or as Mr. Netanyahu put it in his speech to supporters in America, "I bring you a message from Jerusalem, the cradle of our common civilization, the crucible of our shared values. It's a message from the Bible." Then, in Hebrew, he read, "... I have set before you life and death, blessings and curses. Now choose life, so that you and your children may live" (Deuteronomy 30:19).

As legendary Bible teacher, Lance Lambert, recently reminded us, the Jews gave us the Bible, including the entire New Testament with the possible exception of Luke and Acts (both written by Luke, believed to have been a Gentile). And above all, Jews gave us the light of the world, Jesus.

According to a group of rabbis, U.S. Secretary of State, John Kerry, has declared war on God by insisting that Israel carve up her land. (The prophet Joel, in chapter 3, says God will judge nations who do this.) But politicians want to keep pressing, pushing, and squeezing the Jewish people into a corner, ignoring the millions of dollars, euros, and pounds of taxpayers' money being frittered away by the PA whose people continue to live in poverty for which Israel somehow gets the blame.

Meanwhile, Israel's sworn enemy, Iran, is poised to strike as they continue virtually unhindered with developing a nuclear capability. Their military chief has publicly stated that they are "ready for war with the U.S. and Israel."[1] As it happens, the Israeli Defense Force recently intercepted an Iranian arms shipment no doubt destined to add fuel to the flames already raging across the region.

Into this fiery cauldron steps the military might of Russia, now embroiled in a frightening stand-off with its former satellite state Ukraine, a scenario that has serious potential repercussions for the Middle East in general, and Israel in particular.

The Bible (both Old and New Testaments) speaks of a colossal end-time battle over Israel led by Russia.

And this crisis coincides with growing anti-Semitism raising its ugly head once more in the Ukrainian capital, Kiev, whose 200,000 Jews are being blamed by some for the troubles. The Russian Orthodox Church, to its shame, has resurrected the ancient "blood libel" now also propagated throughout the Muslim world in which Jews are accused of murdering Christian children in festival sacrifices—a baseless incitement that originated in Norwich, England in the Dark Ages.

Many Ukrainian Jews are now seeking refuge in Israel, which had earlier welcomed millions of Russian-speaking Jews after the fall of Communism. That was followed in 1991 by the First Gulf War, during which Saddam Hussein rained down Iraqi missiles on Haifa and Tel Aviv (even though Israel was not part of the conflict). But significantly, the war ended on the feast of Purim, which marks the rescue of the Jewish people from genocide through the intervention of Queen Esther at the time of the Persian King Xerxes.

---

1 "Iran's military chief says ready for war with US, Israel," Jerusalem Post, jpost.com, Feb. 12, 2014 http://www.jpost.com/Iranian-Threat/News/Irans-military-chief-says-ready-for-war-with-US-Israel-341196.

Plots to exterminate the Jews have repeatedly been hatched over the centuries and have left Europe stained with blood, but they are ultimately destined to fail. For God Almighty watches over Israel and will come to their rescue once again.

In spite of all this, there is a growing recognition of Israel's legitimacy from Palestinian Arabs. These include the aforementioned Tass Abu Saada, who now loves the Jews—the very people he was once commissioned to kill—following an encounter with Jesus Christ, the Jew!

Bethlehem Bans Baby's Birth!

As Christians around the world focus each Christmas on the image of Mary and Joseph heading for Bethlehem, where Jesus would be born, it may come as a shock to many to consider how this scenario could not have transpired today.

The parents of the Christ-child, for one thing, would not have been permitted to enter the town at all because it is now part of what is known as the West Bank (Judea and Samaria) in the disputed Palestinian territories. (Neither would they be allowed to stay in the proposed Palestinian state including East Jerusalem.) The shepherds and Wise Men—even the stars and angels—would also presumably have had to be redirected to a less offensive location for those currently supporting the quest to rob Israel of much of her rightful land.

The Scriptures accurately foretold that the promised Messiah would come from "Bethlehem in Judea"—in the very heart of Israel, just a few miles from Jerusalem. He came at a time when the Romans were brutal occupiers of the country. Now all this has been turned on its head with Israel portrayed as the bullying oppressors of an Arab minority claiming the land as historically theirs.

Yet through all the centuries after the Jews were dispersed throughout the world following the destruction of Jerusalem in AD 70, the wandering Arab tribes who remained (along with a remnant of Jews) made little effort to rebuild the ruined cities or cultivate the land, which subsequently became wild and barren. Then, in fulfillment of many Biblical prophecies, Jews from every corner of the earth returned to the Promised Land, rebuilt the ancient ruins, turned a wasteland into a fertile garden dripping with fruit and wine and, with their inventiveness and skill, provided jobs from which Arabs too have benefited.

Now we have a massive scrap for land that was previously left untended, threatening to ignite a major war—Israel having inherited a country smaller even than South Africa's Kruger National Park reserved for wildlife! And we have the ridiculous specter of the international community, bowing to the politically-correct pressure of the pro-Palestinian lobby, insisting on still further division of the land to satisfy the demands of a people who never were a nation—a mixture of Arab nationalities who could easily have been absorbed by neighboring Arab states, but are instead being used as political pawns in an international game of chess designed to squeeze the Jewish state out of existence.

It's a bit like the emperor's new clothes. Very few have the spine to stand up and say, without equivocation, that those applying pressure on Israel are actually stark naked. They have absolutely no idea what is going on, are completely ignorant of the historical, Biblical, and legal claim Israel has on their land, and are so poisoned with propaganda and attempts to rewrite history while calling black white and evil good, that they limply give in to its effects as they capitulate to the death of justice and democracy.

And yet there is abundant evidence for all to see of the rotten fruit of Islamic fundamentalism, which is driving the agenda in the Middle East and elsewhere. Israeli citizens do not blow up trains, planes, buses, restaurants, and skyscrapers in a merciless slaughter of innocent civilians. On the contrary, they go out of their way to provide emergency medical help when disaster strikes in other parts of the world, such as the 2013 Super Typhoon Haiyan in the Philippines and the 2010 earthquake in Haiti. They do not destroy churches or preside over the massacre of Christians. No, this is the work of men who are so deluded they think they are performing a service for God by killing those who refuse to bow the knee to their religion.

Meanwhile, there has been a dramatic expansion of Hezbollah's weapons arsenal, endangering the entire population of Israel, while the citizens of Sderot—a quiet, safe, and beautiful town until Israel pulled out of Gaza at the insistence of the international community in 2005—have over the past decade had more than 11,000 rockets fired on them! It's the only place in the Western world where rockets are regularly targeted on civilian communities (with hardly a whimper of protest from Western politicians), yet Israel is blamed for causing the conflict.

One Samaritan (West Bank) town is actually run by Hamas terrorists, with a roundabout made up of gravestones in honor of those "martyred" for the cause, while Arab Muslims are lured into becoming suicide bombers to provide money for the families they leave behind.

In supporting boycotts, the world (and the worldly church) ignores the ongoing incitement to violence and genocide against Israel, not to mention the continuing slaughter of Christians in Muslim territories, with Hamas unambiguously stating that "there is no solution for the Palestinian question except through Jihad (holy war)."

All the while Iran is effectively rewarded for sponsoring terror by having sanctions eased just because its new president uses less bellicose language than his predecessor. But as Israeli Prime Minister Binyamin Netanyahu implies, better the devil you know (Mahmoud Ahmadinejad) than a wolf in sheep's clothing. Is this 1938 all over again, when appeasement with the Nazis saw Britain's Neville Chamberlain return from Berlin with a worthless piece of paper talking of peace?

The reason much of the church goes along with this is because, tragically, they are largely backslidden and ignorant of the Scriptures, with a love for God that has grown cold.

This was hardly the case less than a century ago (long before Israel was re-established) when CMJ asked the question, and I repeat:

> "Why is it that the Christian public today is so deeply interested in the coming return of the Jews to the Holy Land? Because students of Holy Writ know… that a time is coming when 'all Israel shall be saved,' and when the Jews will rejoice in their Messiah, and that previous to the turning of the nation to Christ must first come the re-establishment of the Chosen Race in their own land…

> "It is our duty as a society to send missionaries in and out amongst the Jews, bringing the remnant according to grace into the fellowship of the Gospel, and preparing the nation as a

whole for that great day when the Jews shall 'look on him whom they pierced' and acknowledge him as their Messiah" (Zechariah 12:10).[2]

Simon Ponsonby in his book, *God Is for Us*, a brilliant commentary on the Book of Romans, used an example from the Cultural Revolution in China (1966-76) to illustrate verse 12 of chapter 6, which says, "Therefore do not let sin reign in your mortal body so that you obey its evil desires." Chairman Mao in his folly tried to change the coding of traffic lights so that the color red—reflected in the national flag and his Communist rule book—would be seen as something positive. But it was a potential disaster as people were obviously too programmed to interpret a red light as meaning anything other than stop. "Red is red; sin is sin; stop is stop," the author writes. "And Paul wants us to see red and stop sinning!"[3]

Tragically, the moral traffic light in Britain has turned permanently green, resulting in relationship breakdown on a massive scale along with physical and emotional stress and an upsurge in mental illness as multiple pile-ups drain the emergency services of resources.

And in the midst of traffic chaos, feverish crowds crush into shopping malls at Christmas looking for last-minute gifts for their loved ones but, like the innkeeper at Bethlehem, have no room in their lives for the babe who is the focus of the festival. The Messiah's parents had to travel some 80 miles by foot from Nazareth to be in "David's city" (Joseph's ancestral town) for the census, but the Western world of the

---

2 Kelvin Crombie, *Restoring Israel: 200 Years of the CMJ Story*, 2008, p. 134

3 Simon Ponsonby, *God Is for Us, 52 Readings from Romans*, Monarch Books (an imprint of Lion Hudson), Oxford, England, 2013, p. 190.

21st century seems to have lost its compass—and the plot—of what Christmas is really about.

A favorite carol, "O Little Town of Bethlehem," includes the lines, "O holy child of Bethlehem, Descend to us we pray, Cast out our sin and enter in, Be born in us today." If you want to experience the true meaning of Christmas, simply make this your heartfelt prayer.

Palestinian Propaganda Funded by British Taxpayer

As aggressive atheists accuse evangelical Christians of brainwashing Britain's schoolchildren, Arab leaders in the Middle East are teaching their kids to hate Jews, and that there is no such place as Israel—and the British taxpayer is funding such overt propaganda.

The National Secular Society (NSS) in England has called on the Government to act in the face of so-called "infiltration" of schools by a number of well-established Christian organizations they say are "promoting creationism, miracle healing, and other dubious ideas" in a bid to convert their hearers.

But the Education Department says there is no evidence of this, and indeed I know from personal experience that such groups are not only acting within the law, but are helping schools to fulfill their RE (religious education) curriculum for which they are increasingly ill-equipped thanks to the infiltration of secular thought in society as a whole.

The NSS would do better to invest their time in looking at the Palestinian Authority, whose schools encourage hatred and anti-Semitism and where Israel (with whom they are supposedly seeking an arrangement whereby they can live in peace as neighbors) is not even shown on the map.

And the European Union (that includes the UK) props up this system with half-a-million euros per year! In fact, since the signing of the Oslo accords in 1994, the Palestinians have received more than 25 times more aid per capita than the amount of money donated from the United States to Europe under the post-World War II Marshall Plan, which paid for the complete reconstruction and rehabilitation of the European economy. Put in simple terms, with the money donated to the PA over the last 20 years, we could have reconstructed the European economy 25 times!

So where has all the money gone? According to Calev Myers, founder of the Jerusalem Institute of Justice, an Israeli human rights organization, much of it has been siphoned off to the private bank accounts of the Palestinian leaders. Other funds have been used to stockpile weapons, build the biggest police force per capita of any nation in the world, and, as I have said, to support a racist education system.

Even according to Arabic newspaper reports, PA leader Mahmoud Abbas receives a salary of one million euros per month—more than 30 times that of US President Barack Obama! And his personal net worth is estimated at 100 million euros. PLO leader Yasser Arafat died with investments of over 1.3 billion euros!

All of which makes talk of Palestinians suffering economic oppression at the hands of Israel patent nonsense. What is really apparent is corruption on a massive scale with leaders lining their pockets while cash is not filtered down to support the people they are supposed to care about. So while the World Bank, among others, bemoans the poverty of Palestinians, they ignore the very problem that needs exposing.

Meanwhile, our secular friends in Britain are unhappy that our schools are becoming hotbeds of evangelistic efforts aimed at "brainwashing" kids into believing the world is not simply the result of an almighty accident in a disorderly universe, but created by a loving God. Shock, horror!

Actually, state schools cannot teach creationism as scientific fact, but since RE and Bible teaching supports this view, Christians will inevitably be accused of rubbishing evolution. Anyway, Christian groups only access schools upon invitation, but it seems the NSS would deny children the freedom to decide whether or not to follow a faith, a policy which echoes of Communism and indeed Islamic fundamentalism, if you ask me. It could even be argued that it is a denial of their human rights.

Why on earth should we give these secularists a platform? When did they come on the scene to undermine our Christian forefathers, who set up schools, hospitals, hospices, orphanages, and the like, as they taught in word and deed about the love and compassion of Jesus for the poor and needy?

As for the concept of schools for all, these educational institutions were originally founded by Christians inspired and motivated by their faith to offer the inestimable hand of help for living, contained in the Bible, without which the Western world would never have been civilized. To deny such a treasure to our children would be to consign the next generation to perdition and despair—without hope, help, or purpose in an increasingly evil world.

Battle Over Truth Intensifies

Like many world leaders before him, American Secretary of State, John Kerry, seems to think that if only the Israeli-Palestinian conflict can be solved, all other problems of the area will somehow fall into place. But this is patently not the case. Egypt, Iraq, and Syria, all traditionally hostile to Israel, are in absolute turmoil as warring factions within their own borders threaten to destabilize the entire region.

And there is no evidence that the ongoing, one-sided nature of Israel's political stalemate has taken a new turn. Israel appears as ready as ever to live at peace with their neighbors while the Palestinian leaders seem only interested in sound bites aimed at giving the impression that the Jewish state is the only party not prepared to make concessions. On the contrary, they have made repeated concessions in an ongoing "land for peace" gesture that only succeeds in losing the respect of their enemies who merely perceive this as weakness they can continue to exploit.

Withdrawal from Gaza simply acted as a signal for Islamists to start firing rockets at Jewish towns, and now international recognition is being sought for a Palestinian state on Israel's doorstep, further threatening the security of the only democracy in the region.

EU representative Catherine Ashton talks of the need for better education in Gaza, but fails to address the issue of why their children are being taught to hate and why classroom maps and schoolbooks do not show Israel. But this is all part of an ongoing bid to rewrite history. Basically, there is no recognition of Israel now, and they have no intention of doing so in the future.

A senior Palestinian Authority official, Jibril Rajoub, has emphasized that "all of Palestine, from the river to the sea, it's all occupied,"[4] which clearly implies that he does not accept Israel's right to exist under any borders. The PA's constant denial of the fact that the Jewish people are indigenous to Israel with a history going back more than 3,000 years surely makes a peace treaty virtually impossible.

Meanwhile, official PA Television broadcast a series of moving images while superimposing the words: "Let all religions know that I do not make truces. Let every person know that I do not compromise."

The next day PA TV called for protests against Israel's modern rebirth by planting Palestinian flags in cities across the country including Jaffa, Nazareth, Haifa, Acre, Lod, and Ramle—all located inside Israel-proper and ostensibly not part of a future Palestinian state.

This too reflects the popular sentiment that "Palestine" means all of Israel, and not simply the West Bank and Gaza. The "two-state solution" is widely seen as a practical first step toward a one-state solution—Palestine, following the eradication of Israel. Yes, the PA wants it all—they have said so—and yet still Israel is portrayed in the media as the big bully persecuting the beleaguered Palestinians.

In truth, Israelis are not even "occupiers" of the West Bank as this was originally part of their territory anyway—agreed by the UN and its predecessor the League of Nations, only for Jordan to illegally annex the enclave as surrounding Arab states immediately declared war on the emerging

---

4 "Senior PA Official: ALL of Israel is Occupied Palestine," *United With Israel*, unitedwithisrael.org, June 14, 2013, http://unitedwithisrael.org/senior-pa-official-all-of-israel-is-occupied-palestine/

nation. And though recovered by Israel in the 1967 Six-Day War, the rest of the world duly soaked up the upside-down propaganda which portrayed them as "illegal occupiers." The battle in the Middle East is over truth even more than it is over politics and religion.

15

Church Betrays Israel

Israel's security wall, designed to keep out terrorists, has become a symbol of "apartheid" to those who hate the Jews, but also reflects a church 'sitting on the fence' over the most explosive issue of our times. Oxford-based Anglican clergyman Simon Ponsonby, in his book, *God is for Us,* to which I have already referred, writes, "Anticipation of the return of Christ must shape how we live today."[1]

And I wholeheartedly agree with him. If you have a personal relationship with Christ, and are familiar with the Scriptures, you will know that it is not for nothing that there are some 300 references to the Second Coming in the New Testament alone. And there are many more in the Old Testament (or Tenakh, the Jewish Bible) which, of course, also refers to His first coming as a babe in Bethlehem who was later nailed to a cross for the sins of all who would put their faith in Him, and then rose from the dead before returning to the glory of His Father in heaven where He waits for the right time to make a second appearance.

The knowledge that Jesus is coming soon is the perfect incentive to good living as we try to ensure that He will find us busy working for Him and loving our neighbors. It is also an incentive to preach the Gospel, the acceptance of which

---

1 Simon Ponsonby, *God Is for Us, 52 Readings from Romans,* Monarch Books (an imprint of Lion Hudson), Oxford, England, 2013, p. 373.

is the only means by which people can find salvation and purpose. Furthermore, it serves as a great encouragement for believers, especially those suffering under dictatorial regimes such as the many Muslim countries that make life so intolerable for Christians.

Another reason why this doctrine is so important is because we need to understand the signs of the times in which we live—so that we are not weighed down with fear, and so that we can warn others of the relevance of the Scriptures to the political, social and environmental turmoil we see all around us.

All of this begs the question as to why the subject is rarely touched on in our Western churches. Is it that we are too comfortable in our pews, too cozy with our fleeting middle-class pleasures, or too preoccupied with busy-ness exacerbated by ever-increasing hi-tech inventions designed to save time by sharpening our communication links? Maybe it's because the Second Coming relates as much to Israel and the Jews as anything else. Let me explain: Jesus, the Jew, is returning to Jerusalem, where He was crucified, to rule and reign with all (Jews and Gentiles) who will have acknowledged Him as Messiah.

The Bible is categorical in proclaiming that one of the key signs of His return being imminent is when the Chosen People (that is, the Jews) are back in the land from which they were dispersed. This is now happening after the Romans destroyed their capital nearly 2,000 years ago.

The physical rebirth of Israel as a nation is repeatedly prophesied in the Tenakh (the Jewish Bible, or the Christians' Old Testament). But their spiritual rebirth is also foretold— by Zechariah and St. Paul, among others—and this is being experienced by a trickle of Jews that will eventually turn into a flood when they recognize as a nation that Jesus (Yeshua) is their Messiah after all. Zechariah says they will look upon the one they have pierced and mourn for Him as for an only son.

So where do we find the church in Britain today? Some, like St. James's Piccadilly, effectively take the side of the Islamic terrorists in their stance against Israel, performing a sick stunt at Christmas in 2013 by erecting a 30 ft. long, 26 ft. high "wall" on their premises purporting to replicate the security fence around Bethlehem. But that wall is designed to prevent suicide bombers from destroying lives and fomenting further hatred on some of the holiest real estate on earth—the very place where the Prince of Peace will set up His millennial Kingdom.

Never mind that they are simply being manipulated as a mouthpiece of Palestinian propaganda in a bid to portray Israel as the big bully of the Middle East. It's "politically correct" and that allows them to get away with it, without even having their wrists slapped by the Archbishop of Canterbury, leader of the world's Anglicans. That this church represents such a warped view of Christianity is not too surprising because they take a very liberal interpretation of Scripture, being happy to encourage a homosexual lifestyle, for example.

Thank God there are still many churches who hold a balanced, Biblical view of Israel, which also means that they do not apply standards of behavior to the Jewish nation that they wouldn't dream of applying elsewhere—that Israel should be above reproach in all their dealings, never putting a foot wrong. These churches do see clearly that Israel is still the "apple of God's eye," the most sensitive part of

His nature. As such, He continues to hold them close to His heart with a promise of everlasting love which would be against His nature to break.

Tragically, however, the majority of churches choose to sit on the fence on this vitally important issue, offering the lame excuse that it is "too divisive." But it's part of the clear teaching of the Bible, so how can you afford to skip over it without being found wanting when the Lord comes back and asks why you ignored the plight of His people, surrounded on all sides by fierce enemies who have sworn to wipe them out?

Would you want to be in the same position as the church in Germany who did next to nothing when the "Final Solution" was being enacted? And you will have less excuse than they did, because everyone (through modern media) can see that Israel is in dire straits.

By sitting on the fence, you give succor to those who use excuses like the wall to paint a diabolically blurred picture of Israel, who in truth wishes to live at peace with her Arab neighbors and, for the most part, has succeeded in doing so despite constant provocation. The wall is used as an excuse to help drive home a message of hate toward Israel and back up demands for (at best) a division of territory that is Israel's by right and (at worst) driving the Jewish nation into the sea. There is strong evidence to suggest the latter motive is behind almost every political move made by the Palestinians.

As Israel campaigner Mike Evans has rightly said, "The continued charade that the Palestinians want peace is the flawed foundation that guarantees the failure of the entire exercise. Yet Israel is the one that ends up paying the price of failure. The concessions it is forced to make are never matched by actual changes on the Palestinian side."

And isn't it ironic that the very people who were forced into ghettoes by their host nations in the not-too-distant past are now being accused of persecuting others? Of course, it's merely anti-Semitism rearing its ugly head in another guise.

The Gospel itself *is* divisive if you preach the whole counsel of God. At the end of the day you need to make up your mind if you wish to be a true disciple of Christ, denying yourself and your own desire for popularity and a quiet life by taking up your cross and delivering a message that has always caused offense wherever it is preached, even in Britain where street preachers are now being arrested for speaking against sexual sin.

Has the glory departed from our churches where there is all too little evidence of the presence of God? While Christians play at church, thousands lie fatally wounded on the spiritual battlefield, having given up their search for solace as they despair of finding hope, peace, and fulfillment.

Thank God for Melanie Phillips, the former Daily Mail columnist, who seems to have become a spokeswoman for the true church in the absence of clear leadership from the bishops. In an open letter to Archbishop of Canterbury, Justin Welby, about the St. James "wall" stunt, posted on her blog on December 28, 2013, the courageous journalist charged:

> In a climate in which every Jewish communal or religious event, every Jewish school and institution in Britain has to be guarded against attack, and in which there is a direct correlation between the emotive lies told about Israel and attacks on Jews and Jewish institutions, for one of your churches to lend itself to such incitement is simply obscene.

The "wall" was of course a stunt. But the damage it has done to the Church of England is immense. Because what it does is put the Church on the side of lies and hatred against truth and justice. It has put the Church of England on the side of evil.[2]

There is a precedent for God using someone like Melanie for the benefit of His people. He raised up Cyrus, King of Persia, to help the Jews rebuild their nation following their exile in Babylon. Except, of course, that Melanie is herself a Jew, although claiming only to be an agnostic, non-practicing one!

"The Church Must Repent Over the Sin of Anti-Semitism"

Going back to CMJ's UK 2013 national conference at the Hayes Conference Center in Swanwick, I was soon into furious note-taking when I realized that the keynote speaker, an Anglican clergyman, was onto what I would describe as "a big story." Without mincing his words, Rev. Simon Ponsonby (already quoted) called on the Church to repent of its anti-Semitism, which he described as a sin against the Holy Spirit.

An author and theologian based at St. Aldate's Church in Oxford, he said, "The Apostles would not recognize much in the church today. A Christianity divorced from its Jewish roots has always opened itself up to the demonic spirit of anti-Semitism."

---

2 "A church of hate: An open letter to the Archbishop of Canterbury, Justin Welby," *Melanie Phillips Electric Media Blog,* Dec. 28, 2013, https://www.embooks.com/blog/single/a-church-of-hate,

He confessed to having had a complete "volte face" on the Church's relationship with Israel and that, after reading about how some of the heroes of the faith had treated the Jews over the centuries, he felt ashamed to be a Christian.

He said the seeds of anti-Semitism that led to the Holocaust had been sown by the so-called Church Fathers in the early centuries of the Christian era. Indeed, Martin Luther, much revered as the instigator of the Reformation, played a crucial role with appalling slurs against the Jewish people—even suggesting that the name of their God was to be found in the backside of a pig—which Hitler had merely borrowed. Ponsonby said Nazism was a legacy of Luther, who had called for the urgent expulsion of Jewish people from Germany in his last sermon.

Instead of provoking the Jews to jealousy by displaying the love of Christ, the church has repeatedly caused them offense while arrogantly proclaiming that the church replaced Israel as God's chosen people. Whereas the cross symbolized love and compassion for Christians, it has become a symbol of suffering and oppression for Jews, who have been labeled "Christ-killers" down through the centuries.

Mr. Ponsonby mischievously entitled one of his talks at the conference, "God Became a Jew and the Church Uncircumcised Him," to illustrate how the church has sought to remove all evidence of Christ's Jewishness. Emphasizing that Jesus was a devout, observant Jew who fully complied with the Mosaic law, he said, "You cannot understand the nature of Christ's death on the cross if you don't understand Passover."

Even the Gentile testimony of the day was that He was "Jesus of Nazareth, King of the Jews," a title given both at the beginning and end of his life by the Magi and Pilate, respectively.

Ponsonby continued, "To worship a non-Jewish Jesus is to worship a false Jesus. Any Christology which fails to focus on the Jewishness of Jesus violates our faith and can no longer claim to be Christian."

He pointed out that there was nothing Jewish in the early creeds and even the otherwise saintly Bishop Ambrose admitted setting fire to a synagogue at a time when Jewish believers in Jesus effectively had to renounce their cultural identity at baptism.

"Is it any wonder that we have got where we are today in the twentieth century? What kind of a church is this? I felt ashamed to be a Christian when I read these things. I was appalled and traumatized."

Fortunately the Puritans finally came along with a more literal interpretation of the Old Testament, as a result of which they saw Jews as their "soon-to-be brothers and sisters" whose prophesied restoration to the Holy Land and subsequent acknowledgement of Jesus as their Messiah would usher the return of Christ Himself.

Thanks to the Puritans, the Jews who had been expelled from England in 1290 were invited back by Cromwell in 1655. "And I believe God blessed this nation because of that. Genesis 12:3 ('I will bless those who bless you, and whoever curses you I will curse...') means what it says," Mr. Ponsonby declared.

And when in 1917 the British Government promised to assist in the re-creation of a nation state for Israel, thanks to the efforts of evangelical leaders of the 18th and 19th centuries, the way had been cleared for the Jews to return to their ancient homeland.

Unfortunately, the devil seemed to know more about Biblical prophecy than many preachers, and did his damnedest to prevent this happening—hence the Holocaust.

But what satan intended for harm, God worked out for good, which explains the famous verse in Romans 8:28 that "in all things God works for the good of those who love Him, who have been called according to His purpose" which comes immediately before chapters 9-11 dealing with Israel's falling away and subsequent restoration.

Calling for repentance to God and before the Jewish people, Mr. Ponsonby said the church also needed to renew her understanding of her Jewish roots and reach out to the Jews with love and gratitude as they share the Gospel in culturally sensitive ways.

He believes revival is dependent on our attitude to Israel. "If we turn our affections on the Jewish people we'll see more of God's blessings on the church."

It is undoubtedly true that an enlightened attitude towards the Jews from the Puritans onward led to a revived church under John Wesley and others in the 18th and 19th centuries. And, as explained earlier, with anti-slavery campaigner William Wilberforce among its founding members, CMJ played a significant role in restoring the Jews to the Holy Land by urging the British Government to take up the cause.

Every time Rev. Ponsonby had sought more of God in his own life, he found that the issue of Israel kept coming up. And he believes that "if God can change a stubborn ignoramus like me," He can do the same for others.

Key to Revival: Blessing the Jews!

The search for a key to revival has kept Christian hearts and minds busy for centuries, and many have come up with answers that have much to commend them. Among these, to be sure, is the vital need for prayer and unity among believers, which is what preceded the initial outpouring of the Holy Spirit on the Day of Pentecost, generally credited with marking the birth of the Church.

However, I would like to suggest a related, but no less essential, ingredient which I believe passes the test of both Scripture and history, and to which Rev. Simon Ponsonby has already alluded—and that is the correlation between Holy Spirit revival and Jewish aspirations.

Churchgoers the world over tend to forget (if they were ever aware) that Pentecost is a Jewish festival—also known as Shavuot—celebrating the early spring harvest 50 days after Passover, which marked the freeing of the Jews from slavery in Egypt.

According to the account of Luke in the Book of Acts (he was probably the only Gentile to have authored any of the Bible's 66 books), Jews had gathered in Jerusalem for the festival from all over the known world (Acts 2:5), having been dispersed following the destruction of Solomon's Temple in 586 BC and the temporary exile to Babylon.

The 120 disciples who had been filled with the Spirit as they prayed "all together in one place" now shared their experience with thousands of others who heard them speaking in different kinds of tongues they had never learned, but which turned out to be the native languages of the many and various visiting Jews on pilgrimage.[3] And as a result 3,000 of

3 Acts 2:1-13

them accepted Peter's message that the same Jesus who was crucified in Jerusalem had been raised from the dead, and was indeed their long-awaited Messiah![4]

On all counts, it was a totally Jewish experience, and it was only later, with the help of an extraordinary vision, that God managed to convince St. Peter that the Gospel was also for the Gentiles.[5]

Cornelius was a Roman centurion—a high-ranking soldier of the generally hated occupiers—who prayed regularly, helped the poor and had evidently won the respect of the Jews.[6] He had even built a synagogue for them if he is the same centurion Luke mentioned in his Gospel.[7]

Bearing in mind the crucial verse in the early pages of the Bible—that those who bless the Jews (the seed of Abraham) will themselves be blessed, and those who curse them will invite judgment on themselves (Genesis 12:3)—this God-fearing Gentile who loved the Jews was to be the means of blessing for the entire Gentile world over the succeeding 20 centuries! Peter was still in full flow sharing the Gospel message when the Holy Spirit came on all who heard it (Acts 10:44).

But the experience of the Holy Spirit coming in power, with the result that emboldened recipients spoke in tongues while also manifesting other supernatural gifts, was largely lost in the mists of time as the centuries rolled away. And I'm sure it was no coincidence that this loss of power paralleled a time which saw the church cut herself off from her Hebraic

4 Acts 2:14-41
5 Acts 10:9-29
6 Acts 10:1-8
7 Luke 7:2-5

roots and descend into the darkness which allowed so much persecution of the Jews.

But then, as already mentioned, the Puritans initiated a recovery and the 20th century finally dawned with a renewed focus on the Spirit that gave birth to the modern-day Pentecostal movement, which led in turn to a huge upsurge in missionary activity along with an exponential growth of the church, particularly in Africa, Asia, and South America.

At the same time, the world was also witnessing the rise of Zionism with the likes of Theodore Herzl, an Austrian journalist, promoting the return of the Jews to their ancient homeland partly in response to growing anti-Semitism in Europe. There were also many Christians who sympathized with this view, eventually persuading the British Government to pledge its support for such an outcome. So you had the two strands—new life in the church and new hope for Israel—moving together on what seemed like parallel lines akin to a railway track.

But then, in 1909, a group of 56 German Christian evangelical leaders got together for a conference at which they decided, in what is known as the Berlin Declaration, that the Pentecostal movement, that had its origins in Azusa Street, Los Angeles (1906), and Sunderland, England (1907), was not of God, but of the devil!

In the recently spoken opinion of Pastor Werner Oder, also an Austrian, this amounted to blasphemy against the Holy Spirit, which Jesus Himself said was unforgivable. "They turned out the light in Europe, and we're still paying the price for it," he told a recent conference in York. "The Holy Spirit was knocking on the door of the church in Europe and saying, 'The darkness is coming. I want to empower you to resist the Nazis and protect My people.'"

It is interesting that, despite early success in Europe following the outpouring in Sunderland, the Pentecostal movement made comparatively little impact on this part of the world. But it was a different story in places like Korea where phenomenal church growth accompanied Holy Spirit-inspired Pentecostal activity like speaking in tongues.

Meanwhile, Europe descended into spiritual pitch darkness, allowing the Nazis to exterminate six million Jews in the course of wreaking terrible destruction on all who stood in their way. And though Christians generally did not participate directly in the Holocaust, they did little to help the Jews.

And yet this Jewish nightmare was not enough to prevent a remnant of the chosen people from re-entering the Promised Land, just as the prophets had foretold. And in 1967, following the miracle of the Six-Day War when little Israel (less than 20 years after being re-established as a nation) overcame the might of foreign armies that surrounded them on all sides, the Old City of Jerusalem was at last restored to Jewish hands for the first time in 2,000 years. It was the same year that marked a significant breakthrough of the Holy Spirit in the old established churches through the so-called Charismatic movement, when at last they came to recognize and experience the emboldening power of God's spiritual gifts.

Particularly revealing is the juxtaposition in the Book of Joel of the famous passage quoted by Peter at Pentecost—*"I will pour out my Spirit on all flesh"* (leading recipients into all the truth)—in Joel 2 with a prophecy in Joel 3 declaring God's judgment of the nations for scattering His people and dividing their land. As I write, both the East and the West, led by the United States, are applying relentless pressure on Israel to give up further territory, purportedly in exchange for peace, which it never produces.

Back in the 1830s, according to Simon Ponsonby in *God Is for Us*, Robert Murray McCheyne and fellow Scot, Andrew Bonar, encouraged the evangelization of the Jews, and both led missions to Palestine and Jewish communities in Europe. When a revival broke out in his local parish of Kilsyth, McCheyne took this as a sign of God's promise to Abraham and his heirs that "I will bless those who bless you" (Gen. 12:3). God's favor was on them because they honored the Jews, the apple of God's eye. Like many post-Puritan evangelicals, they believed that the salvation of the Jews leads to the restoration of the church.

Another leading evangelical of the time, Charles Simeon, was similarly convinced about the need for outreach to the Jews. On one occasion, when waxing lyrical with his visions of a return of the Jews to Christ ushering in worldwide revival, a friend passed a note to him stating, "Six million of Jews and 600 millions [sic] of Gentiles—which is more important?"[8] (This was clearly a reference to the Jews representing just 1% of the world's population at the time. The figure today is just 0.1%).

Simeon scribbled back, "If the conversion of the 6 is to be life from the dead to the 600, what then?"[9] (He was referring to Romans 11:15.) The Jews were the key, he was saying. The Gospel is for the Jew first!

Another outstanding evangelical leader of the 19th century, Bishop J. C. Ryle of Liverpool, was passionate in his

---

8 Ponsonby, ibid, p. 301
9 Ponsonby, ibid, p. 301

preaching on the restoration of Israel both to the Land and the Lord. He said, "I believe that the Jews shall ultimately be gathered again as a separate nation, restored to their own land, and [turned] to the faith of Christ [Messiah]."[10] This was years before they began to return in any serious numbers. He also said, "If there is such a thing as gratitude in the heart of man, it is the duty of all Gentile Christians to take special interest in the work of doing good to the Jews."[11]

Another reason for doing so has been well put by Rabbi Barry Rubin who, in his foreword to Lynley Smith's aforementioned book, *From Matron to Martyr* (about a Scottish woman's ultimate sacrifice for the Jews), rightly said, "Jews need to know that true followers of Jesus are our friends."

Best-selling author of *Our Father Abraham: Jewish Roots of the Christian Faith*,[12] Dr. Marvin Wilson of Gordon College, in an interview said, "I woke up one day and all of a sudden I realized everything that had changed my life, everything that was precious and important to me ... all came from the Jewish people." As he put it, "... my Bible, my Lord, my ethics by which I lived, my value system, my understanding of morality, my understanding of what worship and spirituality was about, all of these very important things to my life which for me as a Christian were the things which gave structure to my life and meaning to my life...."[13]

---

10 J. C. Ryle, *Are You Ready For The End Of Time?* Fearn, Scotland: Christian Focus, 2001, p. 9; reprint of *Coming Events and Present Duties*.

11 Ponsonby, ibid, p. 425

12 Marvin R. Wilson, *Our Father Abraham: Jewish Roots of the Christian Faith*, Wm. B. Eerdmans Publishing Company, Grand Rapids, MI, 1990.

13 "How Judaism Helped Me to Understand My Bible" interview, YouTube, July 17, 2012, https://www.youtube.com/watch?v=C60wlGk2wTg

William Wilberforce, who was almost single-handedly responsible for the abolition of slavery in the UK and who was a product of the Wesleyan revival, also championed Jewish evangelism and was among the founders of CMJ. John and Charles Wesley had always supported the idea of the re-establishment of a Jewish state in Israel.

And from what I have managed to glean, Rev. Alexander Boddy, the Sunderland vicar who helped to ignite the Pentecostal movement in Europe in 1907, was also sympathetic with this cause, having visited the Holy Land himself and specifically written articles about the return of the Jews to their ancient home. This is, of course, linked with the Second Coming, about which there was a renewed expectation and interest following the outpouring of the Spirit. Even in the recent outpouring in Cwmbran, South Wales, I believe it was accompanied by good teaching on the place of Israel in God's purposes.

So it's a win-win situation. If you help the Jews, you will revive the church, which in turn will bring spiritual revival to the Jews because they will be envious of the glorious relationship we have with their Messiah! (Romans 11:11)

The connection between revival in the church and the welfare of the Jews is undeniable—a railway track to heaven's heart, if you like. So don't try to separate one from the other. Both these phenomena are litmus tests for authentic Christianity in terms of our spiritual health as individuals, as a church, and as a nation. The Spirit leads us into all truth, but denial of His work results in darkness and judgment. If you wish to see new life among your congregations, consider in your heart whether you are also seeking the peace of

Jerusalem, loving the seed of Abraham, and supporting them in word, deed, and prayer. For if you love Jesus, you will love the Jews!

16

Egypt's Bitter Harvest

Former Egyptian president Mohammed Morsi reaped a bitter harvest for stirring up hatred against Israel. He was thrown out almost as soon as he was sworn in.

The Western media in general completely misinterpreted the uprisings that erupted all over the Muslim world over the past few years as an Arab Spring, suggesting the popular demand for reform would lead to democracy. But the truth is becoming apparent all too quickly that a bitter harvest of growing chaos is the stark result.

The protests in themselves were perfectly understandable in the light of the dark oppression in which many in the Arab world have been held for so long, but they have only succeeded in allowing them to escape from the frying pan into the fire. The fundamentalist Muslim Brotherhood tried to use the call for democracy to gain power before killing off democracy, but the Egyptian people soon saw through their evil plan as Christians and others who refused to toe the line were tortured, or worse.

The reason a largely secular, humanistic, and atheistic media fail to grasp what is happening in the world is that they reckon without its Creator—thus missing out on the bigger picture. As a result, their understanding of political and social movements becomes blinkered by immediate issues they can touch and see, rather than the spiritual realities behind them.

For at the heart of the Middle East crisis is the precarious state of Israel, surrounded on all sides by hostile Arab nations bent on her destruction and about whom President Morsi was quoted in the New York Times just six months prior to his fall as saying, "We must never forget, brothers, to nurse our children and our grandchildren on hatred of the Jews." And he went on to say that such hatred must continue as a form of worshipping Allah!

He was talking of those God has described in the Bible as "the apple of His eye"—the chosen people of the seed of Abraham who would bring blessing to those who bless them but cursing to those who despise them.

Christians Made Scapegoats

And so beleaguered Egypt, until recently Israel's only friend among her immediate neighbors as one of the few Arab nations once willing to be at peace with her, is now heavily embroiled in her own troubles. And though the Jewish state remains the hottest potato of them all, it is ironic that (as I write) she is now virtually the only place in the Middle East experiencing relative quiet.

The friendship with Egypt—the largest country in the Arab world—was also somewhat ironic in view of the ancient rivalry between the two nations which eventually led to the miraculous exodus of an estimated two million Jews who had been held in slavery there for 400 years. At that time the Egyptian army was destroyed as they chased the Israelites across the sea, which had opened up to allow the fleeing Jews to escape before crashing down again on their enemies.

Now the Egyptian military is flexing its muscles again in an apparent bid to appease their own people, who it would seem had inadvertently, as I said, voted to jump from the cooking pot into the oven upon being offered the precious gift of democracy. So the democratically-elected President Morsi was deposed shortly afterwards, leaving Egypt in a worse state even than under dictatorial Hosni Mubarak as Morsi's men vowed to fight to the bitter end to have their man restored to power. The problem was that Morsi represents the Muslim Brotherhood, a hardline Islamist party supporting the Gaza-based terror group Hamas. Clearly this is not what the people had in mind when joining the "Arab Spring" protests in favor of a more representative government looking after the interests of all, including Christian and other minorities.

But now the Coptic Christians, who make up ten percent of the country's 83 million population, are suffering a backlash from those who believe they contributed to Morsi's downfall and have conveniently been singled out as scapegoats just as the Jews were in Nazi Germany. Mobs went on the rampage, setting churches alight while also attacking Christian schools, homes, businesses, and cultural centers. Even a ten-year-old girl was shot dead by an unidentified gunman while on her way back from a Bible class. Most deaths, though, occurred in clashes between the security forces and Morsi supporters.

Targeting Christians in this way, one commentator said, showed that the battle is not for democratic freedom but for spiritual dominance. Local Christian leaders have been shocked by the distorted view of what's happening presented by the Western media, including the BBC, legitimizing and emboldening Morsi's men as victims of injustice because of being elected in a democratic process while giving scant coverage to the destruction of over 80 churches along with monasteries, orphanages, and the like by "bloodthirsty radical organizations."

They ignore the fact that only 13 million Egyptians (less than 20 percent of the population) actually voted for Morsi, who subsequently awarded himself sweeping new powers in a bid to radically Islamize the country and deny rights to minorities including Christians. And all this coincided with the country's infrastructure falling apart, with electricity and fuel supplies becoming unreliable amid soaring prices for basic commodities.

According to human rights activists, the attacks on churches were inspired by "a near-constant stream of vitriol from Islamic leaders calling for retribution against the Copts." Graffiti was painted on church buildings along with Christian-owned homes and businesses declaring, "Egypt is Muslim, not Christian." And to add insult to injury, the Al-Qaeda flag was hoisted atop one church while three others were turned into mosques. Reports indicate that up to 82 churches—many dating from the fifth century—have been attacked.

Undermining democracy may well have been seen as the lesser of two evils. But it was clear that the well-organized Muslim Brotherhood was always going to use democracy to impose its own harsh version of Islam on the people—in other words, to establish a "theocracy" and destroy democracy. The people soon realized their error, but the horse had bolted into the presidential palace,[1] and Egypt suffered for their collective naivety.

Dr. Terence Ascott, a Middle East satellite TV boss, said on August 26, 2013 in a commentary on his Sat-7 website,

---

1 Referring to the idiom: "Don't shut the barn door after the horse has bolted."

"The Muslim Brotherhood have been, and remain, very effective in portraying themselves as the victims to the media, pointing to how Morsi had been 'democratically' elected and that the army 'coup' was a major setback to the country's democratic progress. They have known what buttons to push with the Western press and this seems to be the version that most of the world is hearing—but it is not a version of truth that resonates with the vast majority of Egyptians."

The whole scenario places further pressure on Egypt's neighbor with the Brotherhood stoking up the fires of anti-Israel rhetoric as they tune in to the devilish chorus that seems to win applause from Western leaders. And Egyptian followers of Christ—the largest Christian community in the Middle East—are worse off than before. Will the people of God be looking for a way of escape across the Red Sea as the Jews did some 3,500 years ago?

The prophet Isaiah, writing around 600 BC, said there would come a day when the Egyptians would cry out to the Lord because of their oppressors, and that He would rescue them, after which there would be a "highway" of blessing from Egypt to Assyria, obviously indicating a wave of peace and reconciliation—a modern Red Sea crossing bearing good news. Clearly this prophecy is starting to be fulfilled through events such as *At the Crossroads*. But before its final fulfillment, Scripture also records, "I will stir up Egyptian against Egyptian—brother will fight against brother, neighbor against neighbor, city against city..." (Isaiah 19:2).

Interestingly, Egypt's Jewish population was much greater than it is today before 1939 when a combination of growing Islamization and fear spread by the Holocaust reduced their numbers, with some of the survivors now back in the Promised Land.

Meanwhile, African friends of Israel (including Nigeria's huge Church of the Redeemed denomination) stand in great danger when they put their heads above the parapet. One such individual, a Ugandan pastor named Umar Mulinde, had buckets of acid thrown over him, causing severe life-threatening injuries, after converting from Islam and declaring his love for Israel, a people he had previously hated until Jesus appeared to him in a dream. And although terribly scarred and blinded in one eye, he has forgiven his attackers.

Yet all the trouble Egypt is experiencing pales beside the potential problems for Israel, surrounded on all sides by viciously hostile nations and terrorist groups bent on her destruction. Hamas certainly falls into this category, ensuring regular rocket fire from Gaza in the south, while Iran's proxy Hezbollah is always ready to strike from the north where Syria is temporarily distracted by their own "Armageddon," now being shared with Iraq, as ISIS jihadists threaten to get a stranglehold over the entire region. And with Al Qaeda-sponsored rebels among those trying to oust Syrian dictator Bashar Assad, their guns could easily turn on Israel, the chief target of all fundamentalist fury.

And then of course there is nuclear-arming Iran, where President Hassan Rouhani has already referred to Israel as a "wound" that needs to be removed. So then, not much has changed since his predecessor Mahmoud Ahmadinejad repeatedly called for the Jewish state to be "wiped off the map." Clearly, reports of progress in any new round of peace talks should be received only with a good dose of salt. You would do better to *pray* for the peace of Jerusalem, as the Bible has instructed us to do for thousands of years.

Fools Rush in Where Angels Fear to Tread

The call to respond to the humanitarian disaster in Syria with military action when civil war there broke out was perfectly understandable, but ill-advised. And it was with a sigh of relief that I learned David Cameron had been defeated in his efforts to win Commons support for such a venture.

The sight of so many dreadfully injured victims of a napalm bomb was indeed shocking, and every true Christian should want to run to their aid as in the parable of the Good Samaritan. But though it was obviously clear that chemical weapons had been used, it was less obvious who used them. Everyone seemed "almost certain" the Assad regime was responsible because it was known they had these weapons— thanks no doubt to Saddam Hussein and the Russians.

But the rebels fighting the Syrian dictator are mostly aligned to Al Qaeda and other terrorist groups. What an appalling scenario if we should find Britain and her allies now supporting the very people they set out to destroy following the attacks on America in September 2001?

Quite apart from that, we could not be entirely sure that one or more of these rebel groups hadn't been responsible for this wicked attack on innocent civilians. They certainly have the form, having demonstrated in the past an ability to make a massacre, of their own doing, look like the work of their enemy, thus successfully drawing sympathy for their cause.

As Australian writer, Elizabeth Kendal, pointed out in her report, titled, "SYRIA: Who is Deploying Chemical Weapons?"[2] these tactics have been routinely used in such

---

2 Published by *Christian Press*, christianpress.com, Sept. 5, 2013, reprinted from *ASSIST News Service*, http://www.christianpress. com/world/851-syria-who-is-deploying-chemical-weapons.html

conflicts including Bosnia, Kosovo, and Libya, leading to the intervention of major nations on behalf of Sunni fundamentalist Islamic jihadis. And there is nothing humane about bombing cities and towns full of civilians.

"The fact that the West is so keen to assist and ally with Islamists whose stated aim is the destruction of Jews, Christians, Israel, and the West is short-sighted, irresponsible and irrational in the extreme," Ms. Kendal adds. "It is not only wicked, but is a 'covenant with death.'"[3]

Holding its breath through all this bloodshed is Syria's southern neighbor, Israel, the common enemy both of Assad and the rebels. And the overwhelming worry is that those chemical and other weapons could so easily be turned on the Jewish state, a situation that will obviously not be helped by the intervention of nations seen as "Zionists" by the Islamists at war with one another.

Whatever happens, the ugly truth is that the day seems fast approaching when Damascus will be "a heap of ruins," as predicted by the prophet Isaiah some 2,700 years ago (17:1). Former UN peace envoy, Lakhdar Brahimi, says that without concerted efforts for a political solution in Syria, where 160,000 people have been killed in the civil war, there is a serious risk the entire region will blow up.

---

3   Elizabeth Kendal, "SYRIA: Who is Deploying Chemical Weapons?" *Christian Press*, ibid.

17

"Wolf in Sheep's Clothing"

So it is that some seventy years after six million Jews were slaughtered in the ovens of Nazi Germany, they are in grave danger of another attempt at genocide. But just as happened when Churchill's warnings initially fell on deaf ears in the 1930s, so today the rest of the world is looking the other way pretending such a threat does not exist. This is a constant frustration for those who support Israel, and who understand what is going on, because ignorance leaves people vulnerable to the lies, propaganda, and deception spreading like cancer through the corridors of power.

No wonder ex-Daily Mail columnist, Melanie Phillips, lost her cool in a recent BBC Question Time program over the gross ignorance displayed by a member of the audience who seemed to think that Iran can be negotiated with and their fanaticism assuaged. And even a member of the panel, a Liberal Democrat minister as I recall, was clearly persuaded that the reportedly moderate new President Hassan Rouhani was someone with whom we could do business, to which Ms. Phillips merely gasped in exasperation.

The TV discussion centered round what to do with Syria and the esteemed journalist was merely pointing out that it was their sponsors, Iran, who needed dealing with. We need to cut the ground from underneath the rogue state before they have the capability of firing nuclear weapons at Israel, which they have been threatening to do for some time via former President Ahmadinejad's constant "wipe them off the map" refrain.

Clearly the public seems easily persuaded by press comment that the new incumbent changes the game. But that is to ignore the fact that it is the Ayatollahs who are the Supreme Leaders of the strict Muslim state. Israeli Prime Minister Binyamin Netanyahu, in addressing the United Nations General Assembly, reminded them that Iran (ancient Persia) had not always been unfriendly towards the Jews, but that "Ahmadinejad was a wolf in wolf's clothing and Rouhani is a wolf in sheep's clothing who thinks he can pull the wool over the eyes of the international community."

He also reminded them that from 1989 to 2003 the new president headed up Iran's Supreme National Security Council during which time opposition leaders were gunned down in a Berlin restaurant, 85 people were murdered at the Jewish Community Center in Buenos Aires, and 19 American soldiers were killed when the Khobar Towers were blown up in Saudi Arabia. And now they are providing direct support for the murderous Assad regime in Syria. Yet the West is quick to believe the duplicitous diatribe that speaks of a peaceful purpose for their nuclear program. Mr. Netanyahu is clear, "This is simply not the case. But is anyone listening?"

Meanwhile, the Israeli leader assures the world that he desires peace, but for this to be achieved Palestinians must finally recognize the Jewish state (which they constantly refuse to do) and Israel's security needs must be met.

Yet who are the Palestinians? A Hamas official was heard to ask this question on a live Arabic TV program, admitting that half of them were Egyptian and the other half Saudi. And why do they want another state in Israel when Jordan (originally part of the land earmarked for the Jews) had already fulfilled that role through the 1947 UN Partition Plan? The "two-state solution" much talked about by political leaders today was effectively implemented all those years ago when Jordan was created to absorb the area's Arab population. Why must a state already divided be carved up yet again? The answer, it seems, comes out of the mouth of the same Hamas official quoted above when he said that Al-Quds (Jerusalem) and the land of Palestine (Israel) represent the "spearhead for Islam" in order for Muslims to wage jihad (war).

Protestors supposedly campaigning on behalf of Palestinians show their ignorance by talking of "stolen Palestinian land." But actually the West Bank (Judea and Samaria) was captured from Jordan, not from the Palestinians, in a war of self-defense in 1967—Jordan having illegally annexed the territory in Israel's 1948 war of independence.

There is no Israeli occupation! That is a myth absorbed by a gullible media quick to dance to an anti-Semitic tune as it cozies up to left-wing propaganda. The truth is that Israel is being crammed into a tiny state far smaller than the international community had originally agreed upon, and now even long-term allies like Britain and the United States are trying to carve it up still further, making it smaller yet. Shame on them!

History Repeats Itself

Returning to the question of President Rouhani's alleged dove-like qualities, it should be noted that the leading London-based pan-Arab newspaper al-Sharq al-Awsat reported that his eldest son had taken his own life in 1992 in protest at his father's involvement with Iran's Islamic regime as well as his close ties to the country's Supreme Leader Ayatollah Ali Khamenei. "I hate your government, your lies, your corruption, your religion, your double acts and your hypocrisy," Rouhani's son is alleged to have written in a suicide note. "I am ashamed to live in such an environment where I'm forced to lie to my friends each day, telling them that my father isn't part of all of this, telling them my father loves this nation, whereas I believe this not to be true. It makes me sick seeing you, my father, kiss the hand of Khamenei." The official Iranian press, which is controlled by Khamenei, admitted that Rouhani's eldest son committed suicide but denied it was a political act.

And in reminding us that it is Khamenei, not Rouhani, who runs Iran, Melanie Phillips quoted the Supreme Leader as saying of Israel's Jews that they "cannot be called humans; they are like animals, some of them" and that Israel was "the rabid dog of the region."[1]

"What do you do with rabid dogs?" she asks. "That's right: you put them down."[2]

She added that Iran had been protected ever since their 1979 revolution by a mysterious cloak of denial and paralysis with the West tragically still in appeasement mode. She said the nuclear deal involving an easing of sanctions in return for precisely nothing meant that Britain, America, and Europe might as well go to Tehran and wave a white flag.

"Presented with unambiguous evidence of the Supreme

---

1 Melanie Phillips, "It's 1938 all over again," *Melanie Phillips Electric Media Blog,* Nov. 22, 2013 blog post, https://www.embooks.com/blog/single/its-1938-all-over-again
2 Ibid.

Leader's genocidal prejudice towards the Jews of Israel, the Obama administration merely flapped the limpest of wrists," Melanie writes. "The hostility towards Israel being displayed by the Obama administration is as clear as it is shocking. The rationale being offered by US officials in background briefings is no less jaw-dropping. This is how it goes. Measures to stop Iran from making the nuclear bomb will make the regime even more determined to make the bomb. So it's smart not actually to stop Iran making the bomb. But not stopping it making the bomb, allowing the centrifuges to spin and enrichment to continue, also means it will make the bomb. So it's a win-win for Iran. World loses."[3]

In August 1942, Gerhard Riegner, the World Jewish Congress representative in Switzerland, informed the British and US governments of the horrific plan to exterminate Europe's Jews using gas. Riegner had learned of the plan from a source close to the highest Nazi officials, German industrialist Eduard Schulte. But both governments were skeptical about the information and tragically wasted precious months doing nothing about it. By 1945, six million Jews had been murdered, most of them gassed in Nazi death camps in what became known as the Holocaust—the greatest crime in the annals of human history.

With the spotlight today on Iran, Ms. Phillips writes, "We are indeed now facing the unthinkable. Not just that Iran is on the verge of being allowed to proceed to nuclear capability. The really unthinkable reality is that the enemies of the civilized world are not just to be found in Tehran. They are also in London, Brussels, and Washington, D.C."[4]

---

3 Ibid.
4 Ibid.

However, with the ruthless Islamic jihadists rapidly changing the game, who knows what future as yet unforeseen alliances may emerge? And it is now not inconceivable that the United States will line up with Iran in a bid to stop the relentless onward threat to the entire region of the ISIS terror group as it would be in the interests of both sides to stop them from further destabilizing the Middle East. But it's not a scenario exactly designed to allay the fears of Israel.

18

God's Political Storms

How sad, yet predictable, it was when the mockers came out to make fun of United Kingdom Independence Party (UKIP) councilor, David Silvester, after he suggested England's early 2014 floods might have had something to do with God's displeasure over our sinful ways—with particular reference to Prime Minister David Cameron's redefinition of marriage to include homosexuals. He had pointed out that Britain had been "beset by storms" since the passing of the new gay marriage laws.[1] Tragically, all too few Christians rushed to his defense for fear of being labeled barmy, as UKIP leader Nigel Farage dubbed the man he suspended from the party for his views.[2]

But the much-maligned councilor was not far from the truth. It surely follows that if you believe God created the world (as Christians do), then it is not stretching the point too far to suggest that He might also have some control over the weather patterns, as indeed Jesus so profoundly demonstrated when stilling the storm with a word on the Sea of Galilee. "What kind of man is this?" His disciples asked

---

1 "UKIP councillor blames storms and floods on gay marriage," BBC News, www.bbc.com/news/uk, Jan. 18, 2014

2 "Ukip suspends councillor David Silvester who blamed floods on David Cameron passing gay marriage bill," Independent News, www.independent.co.uk, Jan. 19, 2014

each other afterwards. "Even the winds and the waves obey Him!"[3]

But far more destructive storms have hit our cousins across the pond in recent years, and it is the belief of some, including myself, that this is connected with the efforts of successive administrations to divide the land of Israel—something that is anathema to God if we are to believe the Scriptures.

Not content with reducing Israel to a strip of land smaller than South Africa's Kruger National Park reserved for wildlife, her supposed ally (supported by the rest of the world) has been applying relentless pressure on the Jewish state to give up more land, purportedly in exchange for peace. Proof of its being a failed policy is that, ten years after Israel withdrew from Gaza, rockets are still being fired at Jewish residents from the Hamas-controlled enclave. Was the agreement to pull out in 2005 the cause of former Prime Minister Ariel Sharon's stroke suffered shortly afterwards, or was it simply the final act that broke his heart?

In any event, God has made clear that He would judge those who scatter His people among the nations and divide up His land! (Joel 3:2) Psalm 83 paints an accurate picture of the policy and intentions of Israel's enemies, such as Hamas, Hezbollah, and Iran, who say, "Come, let us destroy them as a nation, that the name of Israel be remembered no more" (verse 4). And the same psalm calls on the God of Israel to pursue the plotters "with your tempest and terrify them with your storm" (verse 15).

So how's this for a string of "coincidences"? George Bush Senior's "land for peace" Oslo Accord of October 31,

---

3 Matthew 8:23-27

1991 was followed the very next day by "The Perfect Storm," as it was dubbed, which ended up demolishing his own home. A year later, on the very day he presided over further moves to push this agreement, Hurricane Andrew—the worst natural disaster ever to hit America at that time—destroyed over 180,000 homes in Florida, causing over $30 billion in damage.

On January 16, 1994 Bill Clinton was mooting with the Syrian president the idea of Israel giving up the Golan Heights (essential to its security), and within 24 hours Southern California was rocked by a powerful earthquake, the second most destructive natural disaster to hit America, behind Hurricane Andrew.

On January 21, 1998, on the very day that Israeli Prime Minister Binyamin Netanyahu was snubbed at the White House by Clinton, the Monica Lewinsky scandal broke, destroying his presidency. On September 28 that year a White House deal requiring Israel to surrender parts of Judea and Samaria was immediately followed by Hurricane George, causing $1 billion in damage. And coinciding with further talks about giving up land two weeks later, tornadoes struck Texas with a quarter of the state declared a disaster zone.

On November 30 that year, just as Clinton had led the nations in donating a massive amount of aid towards the setting up of a Palestinian state with Jerusalem as its capital, the Dow Jones index dropped 216 points as hundreds of billions of market capitalization was wiped out both in the US and Europe. And when Clinton arrived in the Palestinian-controlled section of Israel to discuss another "land for peace" fiasco a fortnight later, impeachment was launched against him over the Lewinsky affair.

Five months later, on the day PLO leader Yasser Arafat scheduled a press conference to announce the setting up of a Palestinian state, the most powerful tornado storm system ever to hit the US, with winds clocked at over 300 mph, whipped through Oklahoma and Kansas.

On June 8, 2001, the day George W. Bush sent his Secretary of State to Jerusalem to promote his "Roadmap to Peace," Tropical Storm Allison hit Texas, the President's home state, causing over $7 billion in damage and closing George Bush Intercontinental/Houston Airport for two days. Then on August 23, 2005, just as Jews were being evicted from their homes in Gaza as part of the "peace" plan, a seemingly insignificant tropical storm slowly gained momentum in the Atlantic and, defying all forecasts with wind strength "off the scale," struck New Orleans with a vengeance, leaving 10,000 dead and destroying thousands of homes in its wake. It was America's worst disaster in recorded history.[4]

As an eyewitness, Geoffrey Grider wrote, "As I saw the thousands of homes destroyed, my mind kept going back to those U.S. ordered bulldozers destroying the Jewish homes in the Gaza Strip. As I saw the thousands and thousands of United States citizens being evacuated from their land, my mind could not keep from remembering the Jewish people crying and literally begging to stay in their land. America found no mercy for the Jewish people."[5]

And, without mercy, Katrina literally "bulldozed" tens of thousands of homes and completely "evacuated" the

---

4 Geoffrey Grider has compiled a list of all these events noted in this chapter, and other such disasters from 1991 to 2005 in his article, "12 SHOCKING PROOFS THAT DISASTER STRIKES AMERICA WHEN IT MISTREATS ISRAEL," July 22, 2014 on *Now The End Begins*, www.nowtheendbegins.com
5 Grider, ibid.

celebrated city of New Orleans. Hundreds of thousands were left homeless, helpless, and hopeless in the greatest ever displacement of US citizens. Around 600,000 jobs were wiped out and estimates put the final bill at over $150 billion.[6]

Are you still mocking, or are you perhaps now more open to persuasion that the Bible is true, and that Almighty God is watching over His own special piece of land? Western leaders are invoking disasters on their people, costing many lives and billions of dollars. Yet no one apparently sees the link with their foolish stubbornness in defying the God of Israel.

We live in a world that has been turned upside down by those who shout loudest—the Islamic terrorists in the Middle East and the gay lobby in Britain—where, just as Pilate finally gave in to the demands of the baying crowd by handing Jesus over to be crucified, our leaders have caved in to pressure to undermine family life by trying to change the meaning of marriage. On that dark day in Jerusalem some 2,000 years ago, the crowd kept shouting, "Crucify him! Crucify him!" And Pilate, intent on releasing Him, appealed to them for a third time, asking, "Why? What crime has He committed?" (Luke 23:21-22)

"But with loud shouts they insistently demanded that he be crucified, *and their shouts prevailed*. So Pilate decided to grant their demand. He released the man who had been thrown into prison for insurrection and murder... and surrendered Jesus to their will" (Luke 23:23-25, italics mine). I know Jesus was *meant* to die, but you get my point. Interestingly, the same passage records how King Herod and his soldiers had earlier ridiculed and mocked Jesus.

6 "Economic effects of Hurricane Katrina," wikipedia.org

The Book of Psalms begins by saying that blessing is the reward of the man who does not "sit in the seat of mockers," but whose "delight is in the law of the Lord" (Psalm 1:1-2). And the Book of Proverbs asks in 1:22, "How long will mockers delight in mockery?" The wicked, the Psalmist says, "are like chaff that the wind blows away" (Psalm 1:4).

It is a dangerous thing to be on the side of mockers. You may just be blown away!

There are two books published in 2008 that helped people start making these storm correlations: *As America Has Done to Israel* by John P. McTernan, PhD and *Eye to Eye: Facing the Consequences of Dividing Israel* by William R. Koenig.

Britain Cursed by Pagan Rites!

David Silvester's comments were clearly not the last word on England's storms, as influential author and clergyman, Dr. Clifford Hill, dropped something of a spiritual bombshell by linking the disastrous February 2014 floods sweeping across the south of England with a pagan ritual during the closing ceremony of the 2012 London Olympics. Dr. Hill referred to the words used—which included calling on "the spirit of water, of open seas and running streams, and of cleansing rain…"—as a "demonic incantation calling upon the spirits of the underworld to flood Britain."[7]

He said it was deeply offensive to Christians, being a serious denial of the God of Creation who has blessed our nation for hundreds of years. "The closing ceremony of

---

7 Clifford Hill, "Storms Over Britain, Who's to Blame?" *Christians Together in the Highlands and Islands,* christianstogether.net, Feb. 2014.

London 2012 was a disgrace and a deliberate insult to the God of our fathers who would be fully justified in saying that we had invoked the spirits of the earth to flood the nation and now we are suffering the consequences." Calling the nation to prayer and repentance, he said, "The storms over Britain today are a foretaste of the tsunami of economic and social chaos that will descend upon us in the near future unless there is a spiritual change in the life of the nation."[8]

The irony (in view of my thesis just outlined that severe weather has stalked every political attempt to divide the land of Israel) is that Britain's David Cameron cancelled his first-ever trip to Jerusalem as Prime Minister in order to deal with the effects of the floods.

Meanwhile, more unseasonal weather—this time in the form of a severe snowstorm in Jerusalem—once again followed the fruitless efforts of the American administration to broker a deal that would further divide Israel. Witnessed by film-maker Hugh Kitson, another influential Christian leader, it was the heaviest such storm to hit the sacred city in decades, and served to totally disrupt the ongoing "peace" efforts of Secretary of State Kerry.

Writing in the spring 2014 quarterly issue of the Christian Friends of Israel magazine, *In Touch*, Kitson recounts that Kerry's "armour-plated Cadillac—known as 'the Beast'—got stuck in a snowdrift" on his way to meet with Palestinian leader Mahmoud Abbas. "The Palestinian police either would not, or could not dig him out, so the IDF [Israeli Defense Force] had to come and rescue him—in Palestinian controlled territory. That was the end of the meeting with the PA

---

8 Clifford Hill, ibid.

President. ... En route to see Netanyahu 'the Beast' skidded off the road and embedded itself in another snowdrift! The IDF had to rescue him a second time!"[9]

He did eventually get to see Netanyahu but spoke to Abbas on the phone with proposals said to have been "unacceptable" to the Palestinians.[10]

And after lambasting his rescuers (the IDF) for their incompetence in not ensuring the roads were passable in the conditions (the snow was two feet deep in parts of the Jerusalem area), he was greeted by further snowstorms on his return to America.[11]

Kerry was trying to "force a deal between Israel and the Palestinian leadership ... which would see Israel lose most of her Biblical heartland as well as her ancient capital city where the Temple once stood."[12]

About this deal, Kitson adds, "Given the Palestinian oft-stated call for the 'destruction of the Zionist entity,' such a deal would be suicidal for the Jewish state that the Palestinian leadership doggedly refuses to contemplate recognizing."[13]

Apocalypse Shakes an Empire

As apocalyptic scenarios go—and we're becoming used to these since TV screens have brought a warring world into our homes—the one experienced about 260 years ago by the people of Lisbon would take some beating. As told by the *Perfect Storms* TV series, the ancient Portuguese capital—then

---

9 Hugh Kitson, "Blessings and Curses in a Snowy Jerusalem," *In Touch,* cfi.org.uk/intouch.php, Quarter 1, 2014, p. 4.
10 Kitson, ibid, p. 5.
11 Kitson, ibid, p. 5.
12 Kitson, ibid, p. 4.
13 Kitson, ibid, p. 4.

the heart of a global empire of vast wealth—was struck by a devastating earthquake measuring 8.5 on the Richter scale.

Much of the population was in church celebrating All Saints' Day on November 1, 1755, when it seemed that the wrath of God came crashing down upon them. As if that wasn't terrifying enough, the quake was quickly followed by a tsunami, as 20 ft. waves flooded the coastal city, and that in turn gave way to a series of fires which made it look like Dante's inferno.

The filmmaker's take on the disaster was that it spelled the end of superstition and the beginning of enlightenment in that part of the world as the camera focused on an Inquisitor sentencing someone to the gallows for alleged "witchcraft." The presumed thinking among the populace went along these lines: "How could God do such a thing to people who were showing their love for Him in church at the very moment disaster struck?"

But the ugly truth about the church at that time is that Portugal and its Spanish neighbor had for centuries been conducting an inquisition against the Jews and all who would not toe the party line on church doctrine, forcing them either to recant or face torture and death, or expulsion. And my own Sephardic Jewish family was among them, eventually deciding to leave for the New World of the Americas.

It's shameful how historians, including the ones behind the *Perfect Storms* TV show, seem to find it so easy to gloss over the treatment of Jews in Europe, as if the Nazi era was a glitch in an otherwise smooth passage for the chosen people dispersed throughout the world following the destruction of Jerusalem by the Romans in AD 70. But the Portuguese

Government has now acknowledged the anti-Semitism which led to the expulsion of much of their hardworking Jewish population, and is seeking to make amends. In fact, they have passed a "law of return" (the only country outside Israel to do so) for those exiles who wish to take up citizenship there once again.

Reflecting on the Holocaust in an article said to have originally been published in a Spanish newspaper in 2008, Sebastian Vilar Rodriguez wrote, "Europe died in Auschwitz.... We killed six million Jews and replaced them with 20 million Muslims. In Auschwitz we burned a culture, thought, creativity and talent. We destroyed the chosen people, truly chosen, because they produced great and wonderful people who changed the world."[14]

He said Muslims had brought religious extremism and death by blowing up trains (a reference to the Madrid bombings committed by Al Qaeda) whereas the Jews that Europe had murdered had pursued nothing but life and peace. "The Jews do not promote the brainwashing of children in military training camps, neither do they hijack planes, kill Olympic athletes, or blow themselves up in German restaurants. And there is not a single Jew who has destroyed a church. Nor have their leaders called for Jihad and death to Infidels (non-believers)."[15]

Yes, thank you, Spain and Portugal. It is time to set the record straight. Let's just hope other European countries follow your example.

---

14 Original source lost. No online source could be found.
15 Ibid.

Menachem Begin Builds a Bridge with Christians

One of the most remarkable advocates for Israel is an American Christian called Dr Mike Evans, whose influence there dates back to the 1970s when he struck an unlikely yet enduring friendship with then Prime Minister Menachem Begin. And it was that friendship that transformed the relationship between Evangelical Christians and the State of Israel, Evans claims. In fact, it was through Begin that modern Christian Zionism was birthed. "He is father of the modern Christian Zionist movement," Evans told me—an extraordinary claim indeed from the multiple New York Times best-selling author and renowned Middle East expert.[16]

Evans originally met the former Prime Minister through Dr. Reuben Hecht, founder of the University of Haifa, who was senior adviser to Begin at the time, though Mike was unaware of this.

Evans told Begin that he had come to Israel to "build a bridge" between Christian Zionists who believe in the Bible and the Jewish people, to which Begin is said to have replied, "Lovely. Let's build it together."

With a Jewish mother, Evans admits that there was initial conflict over whether he should consider himself Jewish or Christian, but it was Begin who encouraged him to stop apologizing for being a Jew and a Christian!

He was at first embarrassed to tell the Prime Minister that, though a Jew, he also believed in Jesus. But Begin replied, "Look, I believe in the Messiah, too. The only difference is that you know His name and I don't."

---

16 This section is based on an email interview with Dr. Mike Evans by the author, April 14, 2015. Used by permission.

Begin even risked political criticism and embarrassment by agreeing to endorse his friend's book, Israel: America's key to survival, reportedly saying, "Don't worry about it. I'm a short prime minister. If I stand on top of newspapers it makes me taller. Besides, today's news is wrapped in tomorrow's fish."

Mike's embracing of Christianity is all the more remarkable in view of the abuse he suffered under his supposedly Christian father who, despite having married one, hated Jews and took out his anti-Semitic hatred on his long-suffering wife who was forced to wear sunglasses much of the time in order to shield her bruised eyes. He was convinced she was having an affair with a Jewish man, and that Mike was the "bastard" result. "So I would sit on top of the stairs crying, watching my mother get hit in the face because of me."

And yet his father attended church every Sunday, carried a Bible and even printed the Ten Commandments on the back of his business cards! Not surprisingly, his mother did not like Christians and, when Billy Graham came on the TV, she would say, "Jesus died; don't dig him up!"

Mike later discovered that his grandfather had been a rabbi in Minsk (Russia) and was nearly murdered when a group of Christians tried to burn down his synagogue as they accused him and his congregants of being "Christ-killers." His maternal relatives subsequently escaped to Germany, only to end up in Auschwitz.

Mike himself grew up amidst constant anti-Semitic taunts and attacks in the largely Catholic environment of Springfield, Massachusetts. And he was just eleven when, following the most brutal ever beating from his father, he finally found the faith that has since sustained him both emotionally and spiritually.

As he tried to protect his mother during one of his father's violent drunken rages, he says his father lifted him above his head and strangled him, almost choking him to death. He recalls losing consciousness and waking up in a pool of his own dried vomit. On regaining consciousness, he said his first prayer, asking God why had had been born. "I didn't see a purpose for my life."

But shortly afterwards, he had a vision of Jesus standing before him. However, it was so bright he couldn't see and at first he thought it was his father—that he must have a spotlight and that he was going to finish the job. "So I was getting ready to dive under the bed to protect myself when I saw two nail-scarred hands stretching forth towards me. And this was the last thing I expected to see.

"The first word he said was 'Son.' I had never heard anyone call me son. Then he said, 'I love you'—again words I had never heard. And the third thing he said was, 'I have a great plan for your life....' It was like a lifeline for a drowning boy."

He subsequently thought of Israel as a metaphor for his mother, whom he could not protect as a boy. He has since faced numerous death threats, but his support for Israel remained undimmed, even challenging former PLO leader Yasser Arafat in person to denounce terrorism at the UN General Assembly in 1988. Holding up a copy of the PLO Covenant during a press conference, he said, "If you denounce terrorism, then denounce this. This document calls for the destruction of the Jewish people."

Evans has recently presided over the building of the Friends of Zionism Heritage Centre in the heart of Jerusalem.

Mrs. Thatcher Saves Jewish Girl from Holocaust

Another significant supporter of the Jews was former British Prime Minister Margaret Thatcher, who was both revered and reviled for her forthright leadership from 1979-1990. Whatever you think of her and despite her many faults, she was undoubtedly a woman who commanded great respect among world leaders. And I've no doubt that the success of her career was in no small measure due to the fact that she blessed the seed of Abraham.

Her proudest moment, she has said, was in saving a Jewish teenager from the Holocaust.

> In 1938, Edith Muhlbauer, a 17-year-old Jewish girl, sent a letter to Muriel Roberts, Edith's pen pal and the older sister of Margaret Thatcher, asking if the Roberts family could help her escape from Austria. The Nazis had started rounding up Jews from Vienna and Edith knew it was just a matter of time before she would be among them. [17]

Grantham grocer, Alfred Roberts, had neither the time nor money to bring Edith to their home.

> So Margaret, then 12, and Muriel, 17, decided to try raising money and asking the local Rotary Club to help. They succeeded in bringing Edith to England where she stayed ... for the next two years before joining relatives in South America.
>
> Edith slept in Margaret's room and Mrs. Thatcher later wrote in her memoirs, "She was

---

17 Sara Debbie Gutfreund, "A Tribute to Margaret Thatcher," *aish.com,* April 8 2013.

tall, beautiful, and evidently from a well-to-do family. But most important, she told us what it was like to live as a Jew under an anti-Semitic regime. One thing Edith reported particularly stuck in my mind. The Jews, she said, were being made to scrub the streets."

In 1995, after Edith had been located in Brazil, she told audiences, "Never hesitate to do whatever you can, for you may save a life." Edith is now a Jewish grandmother in Sao Paulo who says that she owes her life and the life of her children and grandchildren to Margaret Thatcher's family.[18]

Mrs. Thatcher, meanwhile, went on to represent the North London parliamentary constituency of Finchley, which included some very Jewish areas such as Golders Green, and she worked tirelessly on their behalf throughout her career.

When Thatcher visited Yad Vashem during a historic, first visit to Israel by a British Prime Minister in 1986, she was visibly shaken as she stood in front of a photo of a German soldier shooting a Jewish mother and child. She exclaimed, "It is so terrible. Everyone should come and see it so that they never forget. I am not quite sure whether the new generation really knows what we are fighting against."

... About Israel's security, [she said]: "Israel must never be expected to jeopardize her security; if she was ever foolish enough to do so and then suffered for it, the backlash against both honest brokers and Palestinians would be immense—'land for peace' must also bring peace."[19]

---

18 Gutfreund, ibid.
19 Gutfreund, ibid.

Following her death, Israeli Prime Minister Netanyahu said, "She was truly a great leader, a woman of principle, of determination, of conviction, of strength; a woman of greatness. She was a staunch friend of Israel and the Jewish people. She inspired a generation of political leaders."[20]

Mrs. Thatcher's collected memoirs are recorded in her book, *Margaret Thatcher — The Autobiography,* Harper Perennial, New York, 2013.

---

20 "PM, President Express Condolences Over Thatcher's Death," *Arutz Sheva, Israel National News,* April 8, 2013, http:// www.israelnationalnews.com/News/News.aspx/166904#. VRSWILqRPzI

19

Jesus—and the Holocaust

Linking Jesus with the Holocaust has proved to be hugely controversial, judging from the strong reactions elicited from a recent campaign launched by Jews for Jesus, but it is not new.

Artists have taken this line before, and there is even a permanent sculpture exhibition in Israel called *The Fountain of Tears* by Rick Wienecke, depicting the various stages leading to the crucifixion and drawing comparisons with what the Jewish nation went through in the European concentration camps.

For those with spiritual eyes to see, the parallels are obvious. In portraying the coming Messiah as the "suffering servant," the prophet Isaiah talks of his appearance being dreadfully disfigured "and his form marred beyond human likeness" (52:14). All who have seen film footage of the emaciated camp inmates discovered by horrified Allied forces as World War II came to an end—literally skin and bone—will have witnessed something of what the Jewish prophet was writing about.

But then Isaiah asks the question, "Who has believed our message?" (53:1) And this of course suggests that coming generations would indeed have difficulty believing that the Messiah had to die, and in such a gruesome manner, and that this was necessary to cleanse them from their sins. In a similar way, our modern world struggles to get its collective head around what we, the nations, have done to the Jewish people. I've heard it said that it surely could not really have happened, that man is simply not so evil that he would preside over the slaughter of six million innocent men, women, and children in an attempt to wipe out an entire race.

But as Isaiah says of our Lord, "He was despised and rejected by men, a man of sorrows, and familiar with suffering" (53:3). Surely the same description fits the Jewish people over several thousand years?

Isaiah goes on, "Surely he took up our infirmities and carried our sorrows, yet we considered him stricken by God, smitten by him, and afflicted" (53:4). Many "Christians" believe the Nazis were used by God to punish the Jews for rejecting Him, and indeed for "killing" Him, whereas the Bible record is quite clear that Jesus laid down His life of His own accord; no one took it from Him. In fact, the Jews were being massacred because we, not God, had rejected them and in reality it was us, not them, who should have perished in the gas chambers for our treatment of Jesus' brothers and sisters!

Isaiah adds, "He was led like a lamb to the slaughter" (53:7b) Here too is a picture of how the Jews were meekly led away while the world walked on the other side of the road, pretending it wasn't happening.

"By oppression and judgment he was taken away. And who can speak of his descendants? For he was cut off from the land of the living; for the transgression of my people he was stricken" (53:8).

But "after the suffering of his soul he will see the light of life" (53:11).

The devil's plan was for the Jewish nation to be cut off from the land of the living. But God's purpose was that, after their suffering, they would be restored to their ancient land. And so, out of the ashes of the gas ovens, Israel was re-born just as Ezekiel had prophesied in the passage about the valley of dry bones coming back to life. The parallels are not perfect, but they are powerful nevertheless and I am becoming more convinced of the significance of this link.

Author, Lynley Smith, who writes of her relative Jane Haining's martyrdom in Auschwitz (see next section), believes Jesus went into the gas chambers with His people, and took some Gentile believers with Him to comfort them.[1]

It is this same theme that caused such a sensation recently with the 2014 release on YouTube of a video entitled, "That Jew Died for You" by Jews for Jesus who, in their own words, "exist to make the Messiahship of Jesus an unavoidable issue to our Jewish people worldwide"[2] and were established in 32 AD (give or take a year).

The three-minute film shows Jews awaiting selection for the gas chambers at Auschwitz. Carrying his cross, Jesus lines up alongside those selected to die, and the clip ends with the statement, "That Jew died for you," followed by the poignant words that prophesied His death on our behalf:

"Surely he took up our pain and bore our suffering, yet we considered him punished by God, stricken by him, and afflicted. But he was pierced for our transgressions, he

---

1 Smith, Lynley, *From Matron to Martyr,* Tate Publishing, USA, 2012.

2 Mission statement, jewsforjesus.org http://www.jewsforjesus.org/about-jews-for-jesus/categories

was crushed for our iniquities; the punishment that brought us peace was on him, and by his wounds we are healed" (Isaiah 53:4-5 NIV, 2011).

In a BBC Radio 4 interview, Rabbi Laura Janner-Klausner said the video was "disgusting." But her real objection was the idea that Jews who believe in Jesus can still be Jewish, and that Jesus had stood alongside them in their suffering.

On the other hand, conservative rabbi Bernhard Rosenberg, who lost much of his family during the Holocaust, described the film as one of "compassion."[3]

Jews for Jesus communications director, Susan Perlman, explained the reason behind the film in an interview for *Israel Today.* "Jesus has often been wrongly associated with the perpetrators of the Holocaust. In reality, He is to be identified with the victims."[4] Further, Jewish teaching promotes the idea that the death of Jews in the Holocaust accomplished the Kiddush Ha Shem, the sanctification of God's Name. How much more is Jesus' death intended by God for Kiddush Ha Am—the sanctification of the people? It is through Him that we are made right with God (Hebrews 13:12).

Rick Wienecke also sees a connection between Jesus and the Holocaust. Originally from Vancouver in Canada, Wienecke tells in the second part of his two-part DVD, *The Fountain of Tears,* that it was through disillusionment with the

---

3 Bernhard Rosenberg, "Holocaust Remembrance Day: 'That Jew Died for You' is Film of Compassion," *The Christian Post,* April 28, 2014, http://www.christianpost.com/news/ holocaust-remembrance-day-that-jew-died-for-you-is-film-of-compassion-118703/#wjz2wiglHEheB1jk.99

4 David Lazarus, "Jesus Goes to Auschwitz in Jews For Jesus Film," *Israel Today,* April 27, 2014, http://www.israeltoday.co.il/NewsItem/tabid/178/nid/24575/Default.aspx?article=related_stories

"girls and drugs" scene that he began searching for God. "If there's anybody up there, I want to give up all this junk," he prayed in a field one day. "I had this sense that, if I didn't give it all up, I was going to die." He duly came to the conclusion, through a book he read, that if there was a God, he must have something to do with the Jews. So he travelled to Israel and began working on a kibbutz (communal agricultural settlement). In the meantime someone had given him a New Testament and he found himself drawn to the person of Jesus. He became a Christian and despite the generally negative response of Jews to Jesus, who often saw Him as the instigator of all their troubles, he began to see a pattern linking Jesus with their suffering and Israel's re-birth. [5]

Brave Scot Sews in Tears

Just six months before the camp was liberated by the Red Army on January 27, 1945, the life of a courageous Scottish Christian came to a grisly end in the gas chambers of Auschwitz-Birkenau. Her crime was that she loved the Jews! Seventy years after her death, at age 47 at the hands of the Nazi butchers on July 17, 1944, Jane Haining's story came into sharp focus with the publication of a new book.

From Matron to Martyr—One Woman's Ultimate Sacrifice for the Jews is authored by New Zealander, Lynley Smith, a distant relative of Jane, who travelled the world to research details for her magnificent portrayal of this brave woman from Dunscore, near Dumfries—the only Scot to be honored with a "Righteous among the Nations" award by the Yad Vashem Holocaust museum in Jerusalem.

---

5 *The Fountain of Tears* DVD part 2, castingseeds.com, http:// www.castingseeds.com/purchase.html

Jane had been living and working in the Glasgow area before taking on the role of matron at a girls' home in Budapest, Hungary—the boarding establishment of a school run by the Scottish Mission to Jews. She was so dedicated to what she believed was her life's calling that she refused to leave her post when given several opportunities to escape, and even when ordered home by her superiors who feared for her safety.

But more important to her was the safety of the Jewish girls under her care, already suffering under relentless discrimination and persecution even before the Nazis marched into their country. Many of their parents were forcibly split up by the authorities as they sent the breadwinning Jewish men away, ostensibly to work camps, leaving families destitute and distressed.

The children often took refuge in the arms of Jane, who loved to comfort them with hugs and prayers of assurance. When she was forced by new laws to sew yellow stars onto the uniforms of her girls, she sobbed uncontrollably. And when some of the poorer pupils had no footwear, she effectively cut off any remaining ties to her homeland by using the soft leather of her suitcase to make soles for the girls' shoes.

She could identify with those who had lost parents as her mother died in childbirth when she was only five, her baby sister Helen lasting just 18 months, and her father died soon after remarrying, leaving his grieving widow pregnant.

Jane was eventually arrested by the Gestapo on a series of charges which basically amounted to the fact that she showed too much concern for the Jews. Leaving her girls distraught, she was moved around various local prisons before being corralled into a cattle truck, crushed in with some 90 other women in conditions worse than animals would suffer with access neither to water nor toilets for the long and tortuous journey to Auschwitz in south-west Poland.

She died soon afterwards, allegedly of natural causes. But since she had a strong constitution and had held up well even when sharing her food with her fellow inmates in an earlier prison, she is more likely to have been either shot or gassed, like so many of the four million others estimated to have perished at this most infamous of all death camps. A postcard written two days before her death indicated no ill-health, but hinted at her impending "promotion" to meet with her Lord in heaven.

Intriguingly, in a chapter titled "A View from the Summit" early on in the book, the author imagines the scene of Jane's arrival in paradise, which serves the useful purpose of taking the sting out of the horrors that ensue in the narrative. Indeed the Bible speaks of how the promise of resurrection removes the sting of death!

The book has been translated into Hungarian, and the government there has also honored Jane for her sacrifice, even naming an important thoroughfare after her. Yet she had sought no honor in this world except to do the will of God and love His chosen people.

I believe harvest time is now fast approaching as there is a growing openness among Jews, a significant number of whom indicated in a recent US survey that they see no problem with believing in Yeshua and still being Jewish.

As I was meditating on Psalm 126:5—that "those who sow in tears will reap with songs of joy"—I thought of Jane Haining, who wept as she was forced to sew yellow stars on the uniforms of the girls in her care. I have no doubt that the seeds she planted—both in the hearts of her girls and by her own courageous sacrifice—will continue to bear much fruit in the coming days. As mentioned earlier, as Rabbi Barry Rubin who wrote a foreword to Lynley's book said, "Jews need to know that true followers of Jesus are our friends."

The CMJ work was already seeing a significant harvest of some 100,000 Messianic believers at the outbreak of World War II in 1939. Then the Holocaust all but strangled the life out of it. And of course we're still not out of the woods on that front with worrying developments throughout Europe of random, deadly terrorist attacks.

But I was encouraged by the aforementioned speech of Israeli Prime Minister Binyamin Netanyahu also expressing the point that he saw the modern state of Israel as a fulfillment of Ezekiel's prophecy of the dry bones coming back to life,[6] with the re-born nation emerging from the ashes of the Holocaust. But of course Ezekiel's prophecy was twofold; he also spoke of a spiritual fulfillment when Israel would receive "a heart of flesh,"[7] as I have been privileged to share with several young Jews over these past couple of years.

A Suitcase Tells Ten Thousand Stories

A pile of battered old suitcases act as props to a memorial of a very harrowing time for thousands of Jewish children at the outbreak of World War II.

After being snatched from the jaws of almost certain death in the extermination camps of Nazi Germany, the children will undoubtedly have been left extremely traumatized

6 Ezekiel 37:1-14
7 Ezekiel 11:19

by the parting from their parents. And few of those innocent victims could have sensed that it was to be more than a temporary break.

There is a note attached to one of the cases—a particularly large trunk—explaining why its owner had been reluctant to part with it. In donating it to the Holocaust Center and Museum at Laxton, near Newark in Nottinghamshire, England, she recalled how lovingly her mother had packed it, and how it became her most treasured possession because she never saw her again. It left me in tears as I contemplated the pain of that young child, and so many others like her, who had been torn from their mums and dads in a desperate bid to save them.

The suitcases were at the end of *The Journey*, a hugely impressive exhibition vividly recounting what it must have been like for children caught up in the Kindertransport operation which brought some ten thousand youngsters from German-occupied Europe to be placed with British families.

But before the "journey" to England, conducted in a very realistic train carriage with the passing scenery whizzing by, you are led through a typical Jewish boy's experience of what it must have been like living in Germany in the late 1930s.

The sights and sounds of a typical street, complete with clanking trams, are seen through the window of his parents' apartment and you are taken into a schoolroom where he explains via a video screen how he felt when his best friend no longer wished to associate with him because he was Jewish. It's heart-rending stuff, especially when he learns that he is to be taken to England, away from his parents and everything he had known.

There was even a special place to hide in the shop owned by his father, a tailor. The exhibition was really brought home to me a short while later when I watched *The Book Thief*, a powerful movie focused on a German family who kept a Jewish man hidden for much of the war.

Yvonne Franklin, one of many Holocaust survivors who give regular talks at the center, recalled her profound shock over the denial of Nazi horrors when she took her sons to the place in the south of France where she and her family had been holed up during the war, protected by the Resistance. When she expressed her surprise that there was no evidence of that dreadful time, or of the brave efforts of those who risked their lives to shield them from the Gestapo—perhaps in the form of some memorial or plaque—the explanation given was that the events were merely legend!

That is why memorials are so important, because people soon forget, or would rather not remember, and history then repeats itself which unfortunately is already happening in the Ukraine and elsewhere where, once more, Jews get the blame when things start going wrong in society.

Thankfully, they do now have a homeland of their own which was not the case in the thirties, but even in Israel they are not safe as terrorists and their sponsors constantly threaten their very existence.

And as the credits rolled at the end of *The Book Thief*, with my wife and I both dabbing our tear-filled eyes with tissues, I caught sight of a decidedly unmoved moviegoer—slouching in his chair, surrounded by popcorn liberally strewn all over the floor, while he messed about with his mobile. It was the perfect picture of the heartless, ruthless, uncaring world we see all around us that would let it all happen again—if it was up to them!

We need to get off our collective backsides and stand up for what is right!

20

Signs of the Second Coming!

The startling appearance of a bright blue flash lighting up the midnight sky above Indiana in the United States in the fall of 2013[1] is yet another portent of trouble ahead for our planet—and I am not talking about climate change in and of itself. Whatever it was—whether a meteor breaking up or some other strange phenomenon—it was reportedly the country's 13th similar sighting of the year.[2] And serious students of the Bible will be only too aware of the many Scripture passages that speak of such things as signs of the Second Coming.

Addressing the question of how His disciples would know when His return—and the "end of the age"—is imminent, Jesus said, "There will be signs in the sun, moon and stars. On the earth, nations will be in anguish and perplexity at the roaring and tossing of the sea. Men will faint from terror, apprehensive of what is coming on the world, for the heavenly bodies will be shaken. At that time they will see the Son of Man coming in a cloud with power and great glory" (Luke 21:25-27). A parallel passage in the Gospel of Matthew has Jesus referring to stars falling "from the sky"

---

1 "Fireball Shoots Across Midnight Sky In US | Fireball Lights Up Indiana Sky," Sept. 27, 2013, YouTube.com, https://www.youtube.com/watch?v=iCbNN4qC9F4
2 Ibid.

immediately prior to His return. Think also, in the context of these passages, of the apocalyptic Asian tsunamis of recent years.

Furthermore, in all three of the synoptic Gospels (Matthew, Mark and Luke, which cover similar ground), Jesus said that earthquakes, famines, and pestilences would occur with increasing regularity and severity (as with the pains of approaching childbirth for a woman). As I write, Pakistan is burying the dead from the latest earthquake to hit that country which has even caused an island to rise from the sea, with experts predicting it is likely to sink again, calling to mind passages in the end-time Book of Revelation speaking of every island and mountain disappearing as the curtain comes down on the age in which we are living.

Jesus also spoke of "fearful events and great signs from heaven," of wars and revolutions, of deception and false prophets, and of armies surrounding Jerusalem (Luke 21:9-11). In short, the world faces big trouble in the days leading up to Christ's return, and it will be focused on the Middle East where a nuclear conflagration is not a far-fetched scenario.

Among the most significant signs of His imminent reappearance—and this may surprise some—will be Israel and the Church. The latter will be revived with Holy Spirit power, a phenomenon which is already happening in China, Korea, Africa, and South America (and even London has seen a 16 percent rise in church attendance over the last ten years[3]), though persecution of believers will also increase.

---

3 Brierley Consultancy's London Church Census conducted for the London City Mission, *British Religion in Numbers*, June 14, 2013, http://www.brin.ac.uk/news/2013/london-churchgoing-and-other-news/

As for the Jews, they will be restored to their ancient homeland after being scattered abroad for nearly 2,000 years (an extraordinary phenomenon that has been gathering momentum since the creation of the modern state of Israel in 1948) and then, at a time we could be rapidly approaching, they will experience a spiritual rebirth in that the nation as a whole will recognize Jesus—"the one they have pierced" as the prophet Zechariah put it—as their long-awaited Messiah!

Jesus will return, not this time as a baby in a manger, but as King of Kings and Lord of Lords. And it will be a time of judgment as Jesus Himself said His coming would cause "all the nations of the earth to mourn" (Matthew 24:30).

We need to understand and recognize the signs of the times, and be ready to welcome the One who for our sake suffered on a cruel cross, taking the punishment for sin that we deserved.

The stars are one such sign—and I don't mean horoscopes, a strictly forbidden means of seeking guidance or assurance. But if you gaze at the wonder of the stars above and recognize the Creator of the universe as the One who has come down to live amongst us, He will hear even your smallest prayer.

Blood Moon Could Mean War on Earth

But it's not just about the stars. A "world-shaking event"—possibly of apocalyptic proportions—is taking place in 2014-2015, according to American preacher John Hagee.

His premise is based on lunar eclipse predictions by NASA, which coincide with Jewish festivals as well as echoing many Biblical passages relating to events described as signs of the imminent return of Jesus.

NASA (America's National Aeronautical Space Association) has apparently predicted a succession of four blood moons—that is, when an eclipse turns the moon blood-red—which happened to fall on the key Jewish feasts of Passover and Tabernacles in both years. And three of these four consecutive blood moons have already appeared—on April 15, 2014 and October 8, 2014 and April 10, 2015—over parts of the globe.

Such a phenomenon, we are told in the recorded "The Coming Four Blood Moons" sermon of Rev. Hagee's, has only occurred three times in the past 500 years—in 1492, 1948 and 1967—and each occasion has been highly significant for the Jewish people. Traditionally, blood moons are portents for Israel, representing both tears and triumph, as was experienced on all three of these dates: the expulsion of Jews from Spain in 1492 followed by the discovery of America by the Italian Jew Christopher Columbus, the re-birth of Israel in 1948 following the bid to exterminate the Jews in the Holocaust, and the Six-Day War of 1967 when Jerusalem was restored into Jewish hands for the first time in 2,000 years.

The significance of Passover (or Pesach) is that it is a celebration of Jewish freedom from slavery in Egypt while the Feast of Tabernacles (or Sukkot) is a time when Jews give thanks for God's protection of Israel in the wilderness.

NASA has also predicted that, sandwiched between these blood moons, there will be a total eclipse of the sun which scholars say traditionally relates to God's judgment on the wider world.

As I've already said, Jesus predicted that there would be signs from heaven in the days immediately preceding his coming again. Rev. Hagee calls it "God's billboard" through which the Almighty will be literally screaming at the world, "I am coming soon!"

He was adamant, however, that he was not predicting a date for the Second Coming, but that we should respond to this "massive demonstration from the heavens" by ensuring that we are ready for it.

Speculating on the significant event to which such a sign might refer, he reminds us of prophecies from Ezekiel and the Book of Revelation in which Russia forms an alliance with Arab and other Middle Eastern countries in an all-out attack on Israel, leading to a mighty conflagration that would see their huge armies routed against all odds, so much so that it would take seven months to bury their dead. The attack would be launched when the combined armies perceive that Israel is unprotected (i.e. when America can no longer be guaranteed to back them). As a result, Israel would know that God is their refuge, not Washington, as their enemies are wiped out like Pharaoh's army in ancient Egypt.

The world's overall rejection of Christ, Rev. Hagee adds, is paving the way for the rise of the Antichrist "who will make Adolf Hitler look like a choirboy" as all hell literally breaks loose.

Speaking of the time that would indicate His coming is imminent, Jesus quotes from Isaiah: "The sun will be darkened, and the moon will not give its light; the stars will fall from the sky, and the heavenly bodies will be shaken" (Matthew 24:29). And the prophet Joel said something similar, which was evidently so important that it was quoted by St. Peter on the Day of Pentecost, "I will show wonders in the heavens and on the earth, blood and fire and billows of smoke. The sun will be turned to darkness and the moon to blood before the coming of the great and dreadful day of the Lord" (Joel 2:30-31).

These apocalyptic events will evidently include both war on the ground and signs in the heavens as a final warning to prepare for a day that will be "great" for those who are ready but "dreadful" for those who have not bowed the knee to Jesus.

The Great Tribulation

Yes, we are living in horrendous times. I don't understand why horror movies are so popular, because you don't have to go near the cinema to witness nightmare scenarios.

Take the Christians in Iraq, Syria, and elsewhere in the Muslim world, for example. Their lives are in constant danger—yes, just for believing in Jesus—and even as I write, countless beautiful people, living good lives and loving their neighbors, are being hounded and persecuted, and even brutally put to death.

Two young girls witnessed the public beheading in Somalia of their mother and her cousin by Al Shabaab Islamic terrorists seeking to wipe out any trace of Christians from their area, with the youngest screaming and shouting for someone to save her mum. These are the same terrorists who killed 67 people in the shopping mall attack in Nairobi. I also heard how gunmen, probably from the same group, sprayed a congregation with bullets, killing seven and leaving others critical, after entering a Sunday morning worship service at the Joy in Jesus Church in Mombasa on the Kenyan coast. And then there is the ongoing murder and mayhem being unleashed in Nigeria by Boko Haram, another Al Qaeda-type group, in which hundreds, if not thousands, of

Christians have been slaughtered in recent days. And similar atrocities are being carried out in Syria, Iraq, Iran, and many other dark places.

There are YouTube films of Christians being beheaded for their faith; I do not encourage you to watch these as a friend who has done so has since had recurring nightmares. But you perhaps need to grasp the reality in which so many are living. This is not the fantasy world of escapist movies, but the heavy price being paid by thousands for following Jesus, about which He did warn, "You will be handed over to be persecuted and put to death, and you will be hated by all nations because of me" (Matthew 24:9).

One video clip shows the beheading of a church leader and his two assistants. Another shows a Christian teenager being gang-raped in the streets of Cairo and, while the perpetrators scream, "Allahu Akbar," Muslim women walk past without protesting.

We talk glibly about rights in the Western world, but these folk are even denied the right to live by a religion intolerant of anyone who does not subscribe to its tenets.

Some naïve churchgoers talk as if we all worship the same God, in which case can they please explain why Christians are being martyred for their faith in so many Muslim lands? And then there is North Korea, a ghastly relic of old communism that brooks no hint of opposition and where believers face the prospect of execution.

The Bible refers to a time in the days immediately preceding the Second Coming of Christ as the Great Tribulation, a seven-year period in which believers will be subjected to torture on an unprecedented scale. There is even a mention of "those who had been beheaded because of their testimony for Jesus" coming back to life at the judgment

(Revelation 20:4). It would seem that, as I write, our brothers and sisters in Muslim and Communist lands are already experiencing this Great Tribulation, as are some of our brothers and sisters here in Britain—I know people who have suffered nightmarish years of stress as a result of false accusation, and one of our most outstanding Christian leaders faces a similar predicament. Christians in Britain generally are rapidly becoming persona non-grata, being marginalized into the fringes of society where they can be ignored, ridiculed, and written off as crazy bigots. Some are even being arrested.

But who is speaking out? What is our government doing to protest about the persecution of Christians? Our media rarely gives it more than a few column inches, and the church is largely silent and asleep.

We dare not remain silent. Each year the Jewish people celebrate the feast of Purim, which marks their rescue from a plot to exterminate them nearly five centuries before Christ. Only the intervention of Queen Esther, the beautiful Jewish wife of the Persian King Xerxes, prevented the catastrophe. She had been warned by her uncle and guardian, Mordecai, that keeping quiet about it would be no guarantee she would escape the genocide herself. He suggested that her royal position may well have been "for such a time as this" (Esther 4:14).

Behind the plot was Haman, the king's chief minister, and there is a group with a very similar name today—Hamas—which still threatens to destroy the Jewish people. Haman had said to King Xerxes, "There is a certain people dispersed and scattered among the peoples in all the provinces of your kingdom whose customs are different … it is not in the king's best interest to tolerate them" (Esther 3:8).

Likewise Hamas, and indeed many within the Arab/Muslim world, will simply not tolerate the Jewish nation because, for one thing, they stand in the way of complete Islamic rule in the most strategic part of the world. And this is what the battle is all about. It has little to do with injustice suffered by the Palestinian people and everything to do with Islamic rule.

There is a hotel in Bethlehem, where our Lord was born and where the anti-Israel, pro-Palestinian "Christian" conference "Christ at the Checkpoint" (bi-annual since 2012) has been held, which has swastikas carved into its façade. It's a chilling reminder of the anti-Semitism that is behind much of what the mainstream media seem happy to absorb, as the conference acts as a propaganda mouthpiece for the notion that Palestinians are being bullied by Israel.

We can choose to remain silent and complacent or, like Esther, we can decide to act and advocate for the rights and protection of both Christians and Jews.

There's so much pressure to compromise our faith. But don't give in, refuse to remain silent, speak up and preach the Good News without which all hell will continue to break loose. The Gospel of Jesus, the Jew, offers the only hope to the world's troubles, the only solution to our personal suffering and pain. Keep faith with Jesus—for His sake, for your sake, and for the sake of your brothers and sisters facing severe trials.

Secularists Succumb to Islamic Barbarism

The outrageous brutality being meted out in the name of justice by various Islamic regimes almost defies belief. But it's heartening that at last the mainstream media did take up the cause in defense of people like Meriam Ibrahim, the Sudanese Christian woman sentenced to death (but only after

100 lashes) for adultery and apostasy until the authorities succumbed to international condemnation and, no doubt, the prayers of many. The baby to which Meriam gave birth in prison was deemed illegitimate because her husband, Daniel, is not Muslim, and their marriage is not recognized because she allegedly *converted* to Christianity, whereas, in fact, she was brought up a Christian.

Though Meriam's case was particularly shocking, she is not alone in suffering at the hands of a fanatical religion that naïve Western leaders still insist on defending as "peace-loving." As I have just briefly outlined, there are Christians facing the death penalty for their faith in Muslim countries all over the world—I recently heard of crucifixions being carried out in Syria—but so far little is being done to protest against these barbaric policies.

In Pakistan, a pregnant woman was stoned to death for marrying the man she loved against her family's wishes. She was allegedly murdered in broad daylight—and in full view of Lahore's high court—by 20 members of her own family in what is known as an "honor killing."[4] And while all this is going on, the UK is demonstrating a growing tolerance and even acceptance of Sharia Law—the harsh form of justice demanded by Islam.

As religious liberty expert Elizabeth Kendal points out, rulings such as that of the Khartoum court in the case of Meriam are totally consistent with Islam, and she quotes

---

4 "Stoned to death for marrying the man she loved...." *Daily Mail.com,* May 27, 2014, http://www.dailymail.co.uk/news/article-2640632/Stoned-death-marrying-man-loved-Woman-attacked-sticks-bricks-20-members-OWN-family-broad-daylight-Pakistan.html

from the famous Hadith, the sayings of Muhammad, that whoever changes his Islamic religion must be killed.[5]

And don't be tempted to think that these are only issues you might face in some far-off country, because former Muslims who have found peace in Jesus Christ are being persecuted in Britain too! The problem is that those who govern and influence us have succumbed to the intimidating tactics of Islam either because they are spineless or because they are ignorant of Christianity—or perhaps both. Even some of our churches are too scared to face up to this threat for fear of causing offense, or of being persecuted themselves.

By contrast, did Jesus ever force anyone to follow Him? And when St. Peter cut off a soldier's ear with his sword during the arrest of his Master, he was roundly rebuked with the words, "Those who live by the sword will die by the sword" (Matthew 26:52 paraphrased). Our Lord was then whipped and beaten almost to a pulp before being nailed to a wooden cross and hoisted up to die a cruel death. And what was His response? "Father, forgive them, for they do not know what they are doing!" (Luke 23:34)

Thanks to the influence of the Methodist missionaries responsible for his education, South Africa's legendary president Nelson Mandela was able to reflect this same attitude against those who had imprisoned him for 27 years and inflicted such harsh discrimination on his people. In the same way, the saintly Dutchwoman Corrie ten Boom was able to forgive the guard responsible for the murder of her sister in a German concentration camp.

---

5 Elizabeth Kendal, "Sudan: Khartoum's rulings are totally consistent with Islam," *Christian Liberty Monitoring,* May 20, 2014, http://elizabethkendal.blogspot.com/2014/05/sudan-khartoums-rulings-are-totally.html

Eric Lomax suffered severe brutality at the hands of a Japanese officer during the building of the Burma railway by British prisoners-of-war following the fall of Singapore in 1942. His torture was so severe that he was unable to speak about it until much later in life, and then only through the encouragement and perseverance of his adoring wife.

His story is powerfully told in *The Railway Man*, starring Colin Firth and Nicole Kidman. I don't know what sort of faith he had, but he was eventually, somehow, able to dig into deep spiritual reserves as he tracked down his persecutor with initial intentions of wreaking revenge. Instead he forgave him, and they subsequently became great friends!

Eric was an incredibly brave young officer. The beatings he endured were the result of his owning up to "offenses" actually committed by his colleagues—the very picture of what Jesus has done for us in dying in our place for our sins. And at the conference in Israel, I witnessed Arab and Jew embracing one another because of their mutual love for Jesus! Remember Ali, who went on a pilgrimage to Mecca to get his life straightened out, but instead discovered Jesus, who told him to "leave this place."

It may be politically incorrect to say so, but Jesus teaches us that there is light—and there is darkness. He did not encourage us to shop in a pick-n-mix religious supermarket bristling with aisles in various shades of light. He Himself is the Light, and all other ways lead to darkness. He said, "The thief comes only to steal and kill and destroy; I have come that they may have life, and have it to the full" (John 10:10). Where there is neither mercy nor justice, but only persecution of Jews and Christians—that's the devil's domain; don't go there!

A lovely Jewish lady I met in Jerusalem summed up the difference between Islam and Judeo-Christianity by saying that while the former worships death, the latter loves and values life. Violence is endemic and suicide bombers are remembered with great honor in Islamic communities. But even secular Israelis are going the extra mile by treating victims of the civil war in neighboring Syria, operating on Arab babies with heart defects, and being the first to respond to disasters in other parts of the world.

Jesus said, "I am the way and the truth and the life. No-one comes to the Father except through me" (John 14:6).

Jesus Still Heals in Israel

Although increasing darkness will engulf us as Jesus' return draws near, there will also be shafts of light. For the Holy Spirit will be poured out on all flesh, as the prophet Joel foretold, and all who call on the name of the Lord will be saved. The "day of the Lord" will be "dreadful" for those who refuse to respond to Jesus, but "great" for those who are drawn to His light. (See Joel chapter 2.)

In this respect, we are seeing a softening of hearts in Israel itself, as I have witnessed, and many Israelis learned in 2014 of an amazing miracle in their midst. For when Therese Daoud arrived at Tel Aviv's Ichilov Hospital with a huge cancerous tumor on her leg, doctors said that amputation was her only hope of survival.

But what happened over the next few months left medical staff speechless. After her radical operation was postponed for the third time—there were technical difficulties, other emergencies, and then her mother became very sick—the junior high school science teacher took it as a "clear sign from heaven" that she was simply to trust God through prayer in Jesus. As a result, a malignant tumor the size of an orange dramatically receded until there was no sign of cancer.

"If someone had told me the story of what happened to Therese, I would have said they are crazy and sent them to a mental hospital," Professor Yaakov Bickels, head of the hospital's orthopedic-oncology department, told Israel's Channel 2. "But I was there. I saw it with my own eyes." [6]

He explained, "This is one of the most aggressive and terrifying of all cancerous tumors. With a tumor developed to this degree, the only treatment we could offer Therese was to amputate her leg."

Lab tests and x-rays were sent to the USA to double-check, but they came back with the same prognosis.

"When she told me that she had decided not to have the leg amputated, it was clear to me. She would soon die," Bickels said. "I was sorry about her decision."

Three months later, wearing a huge smile on her face, Therese walked unaided into the professor's office. And when asked what had happened, she responded, "I prayed."

She was immediately sent for a scan, and the results were undeniable. The growth had receded considerably and another biopsy revealed the cancer had completely left her body.

"We kept checking her records over and over," said an astonished Bickels. "We just could not accept that the cancer

---

6 See the Hebrew newscast here: http://www.mako.co.il/news-is-rael/health/Article-698139f89a95341004.htm?sCh=3d385dd2d d5d4110&pId=1434139730

had gone without any treatment."[7] Israeli TV showed images of her praying in a church in the north of the country.

Hospital staff and news reporters even travelled to Therese's home to look for some other explanation, but were apparently forced to acknowledge it was a miracle wrought by Yeshua, the same Messiah who went about healing the sick of Israel some 2,000 years ago!

"Messiah Appears to Famous Rabbi"

Something else very remarkable has taken place in Jerusalem of late, so I've heard, concerning a certain Rabbi Yitzhak Keduri, who died in 2006 aged over a hundred and drew some 300,000 people (more than a third of the city's population) to a funeral held within 24 hours of his death! The story goes that, just a month before his passing, Yitzhak had a dream in which Mashiach (the Messiah) appeared to him, revealing his name![8] The famous rabbi apparently wrote it down and placed it in an envelope with instructions for his family to open it a year after his death. I'm told that the name he wrote down was "Yeshua," whom the rabbi believed would appear (presumably in a more general sense) after the death of Ariel Sharon, Israel's former Prime Minister and legendary war hero who suffered a stroke on January 4, 2006 and remained in a coma for eight years until he finally died in

---

7 Read about it in English in *Israel Today:* http://www.israeltoday. co.il/NewsItem/tabid/178/nid/24348/Default.aspx?article=related_stories or in *The Blaze* which includes x-rays of her leg: http://www.theblaze.com/stories/2014/01/05/a-gift-from-god-woman-and-her-doctor-say-prayer-miraculously-healed-her-malignant-cancerous-tumor/

8 Aviel Schneider, "The Rabbi, the Note and the Messiah," *Israel Today,* May 30, 2013, reprint of cover story, April 2007 issue of *Israel Today Magazine,* http://www.israeltoday.co.il/NewsItem/ tabid/178/nid/23877

January 2014. The identity of Israel's Messiah, as Menachem Begin indicated in his conversation with Dr. Mike Evans (see chapter 18), is evidently something of a missing link for many Jews. But it will become clearer for them as the time of his return draws closer.

Make of the rabbi's story what you will, but there is growing evidence that Yeshua will soon place His feet on the Mount of Olives, from where He ascended 2,000 years ago. Billy Graham's daughter, Anne Graham-Lotz, certainly thinks so, and she is a highly-respected, sane figure in the Christian world. Warning that judgment is coming and issuing an urgent call to prayer, she believes we are racing toward a dramatic conclusion to world events. "One of the things [God] has impressed on me is that we are living at the end of human history as we know it," she said.[9]

9 "Anne Graham Lotz Sounds Alarm, Calls for Prayer," CBN News, July 4, 2014, http://www.cbn.com/cbnnews/us/2014/July/Anne-Graham-Lotz-Sounds-Alarm-Calls-for-Prayer/.)

21

The Passover Lamb

The annual Passover feast celebrated by Jews everywhere has deep significance for all people throughout the ages. It marks the time when the Israelites were freed from slavery in Egypt by God's miraculous intervention. But there was something they had to do in order to claim that freedom for their particular family, and that was to daub the lintels and doorposts of their houses with the blood of a lamb sacrificed for the occasion.

The stubborn Pharaoh had opened up his country to a succession of dreadful plagues by refusing to let God's people go until finally, with drastic action now required, the Angel of Death was called upon to strike the firstborn of Egypt.

God's chosen people were spared, however, as the angel "passed over" those who had obeyed the Lord's instructions through Moses by marking their doorways with the lamb's blood as they ate their meal in a hurry with unleavened bread (which hasn't had time to rise). They were all packed up and ready to make their flight to freedom through the miraculous crossing of the Red Sea.

And more than a thousand years later, it was at the feast of Passover that Jesus was crucified for our sins—his cousin, John the Baptist, having declared a few years earlier, "Look, the Lamb of God, who takes away the sin of the world" (John 1:29).

Jesus, a Jewish rabbi, had Himself celebrated Passover with His disciples shortly before His trial after booking a large Upper Room for the occasion. And in doing so He instituted what has become known to Christians as Holy Communion.

But it was a Passover meal much like that celebrated by Jews today, except that when it came to the third of the traditional four cups of wine poured out (known as the "cup of redemption"), He made the startling declaration, "This is My blood of the new covenant, which is poured out for many for the remission of sins" (Matthew 26:28 NKJV). "This do, as often as you drink it, in remembrance of Me" (1 Corinthians 11:25b NKJV).

He was about to be sacrificed as the ultimate Passover Lamb, of which all previous feasts were only a foretaste. And He added that He would not drink again of the fruit of the vine "until that day when I drink it anew in the kingdom of God" (Mark 14:24).

This was powerfully brought home to us in a dream my wife experienced in which she understood that He cannot drink wine until we are all together at what is described in the Bible as the "marriage supper of the Lamb."

Jesus also broke bread and gave it to His disciples, saying, "This is my body," so inaugurating the regular feast of bread and wine celebrated around the world by two billion Christians today.

The unleavened bread used by Jews today (Matzos) is full of tiny holes, with darker stripes on the back, reflecting I'm sure that the body of Jesus was pierced by cruel nails holding him to the cross while his back was as a ploughed field beaten by whips.

The prophet Isaiah surely prophesied about this day when he said, "He was pierced for our transgressions, he was crushed for our iniquities; the punishment that brought us peace was upon him, and by his wounds we are healed" (Isaiah 53:5).

Possibly with the cross in mind, Moses was instructed to tell the Israelites that the Lord would redeem His people "with an outstretched arm" (Exodus 6:6) and the psalmist adds that "with a mighty hand and outstretched arm" God's love endures forever (Psalm 136:12).

As He hung in agony of soul and body on that cross outside Jerusalem, Jesus accepted the offer of a final drink from a soldier who, significantly, used the stalk of a hyssop plant to dip a sponge in a jar of wine vinegar with which to wet the lips of the Messiah. The Israelites had been instructed to use hyssop to daub the lamb's blood on their doorposts before leaving Egypt. And was Jesus partaking of the fourth cup— the cup of completion—before declaring "It is finished" and breathing his last?

All those wishing to have their sins "passed over" must avail themselves of the precious blood of Jesus, figuratively "marking" it on their hearts as protection from eternal destruction and a guarantee of life everlasting. As the hymn-writer said, "There was no other good enough to pay the price of sin. He only could unlock the gate of heaven and let us in"[1]

Whatever you do at Passover—or Easter, nothing comes anywhere near the importance of what you do with Jesus (Yeshua). Will you let Him in by figuratively marking your heart and life with His atoning blood?

---

1 From the hymn, "Christ Dying to Save Us," Cecil Frances Alexander, 1848.

Christianity Cannot Exist Without Judaism

I have spent many happy hours helping my niece and nephews build sandcastles on the beaches of the beautiful Yorkshire coast, and more recently in Cornwall. But as you too will no doubt have discovered for yourself, the structure turns out to be all too temporary. For when the tide comes in, our best efforts are left in ruins, and the kids are sometimes left in tears. But of course it was great fun while it lasted.

If we're building a real castle, however, we need to build on a stronger foundation, and that also goes for the Christian faith. In fact, everything depends on the nature of this foundation. Otherwise our world may well collapse around us when the incoming tide overwhelms us, and we are left rudderless, insecure, and lost on the ocean wave of a life without apparent direction or hope.

There is a teaching gaining ground in some church circles—partly influenced, I suspect, by a wish to appease militant Islam—that Christians have replaced Jews as God's chosen people. I mentioned it earlier. Those who spread this view attribute the Biblical promises and prophecies about Israel as now applying solely to the Church—the "new Israel" as they see it. Yet numerous such Old Testament prophecies speak of Jews—dispersed among the nations for 2,000 years—returning to their ancient homeland in the last days. And the entire world has witnessed this phenomenal event over the last 66 years—since Israel was re-born as a modern state in 1948.

How can this possibly relate to Christians, who have never had an earthly homeland of their own? Perhaps the suggestion is that these Scriptures speak of believers eventually finding their own Promised Land in heaven? But the word "restore" or "return" makes nonsense of this as they were not God's people before they became Christians!

The truth is that Christianity is a fulfillment of Judaism, and Jesus is a fulfillment of all the Old Testament prophecies and Jewish feasts, the ultimate Passover Lamb taking our sins upon Himself, first for the Jew and also for the Gentile. The sacrificial blood of Christ, which we symbolically share in the communion wine, was prefigured by the blood of the lamb on the doorposts of the houses of the enslaved Jews of Egypt. The Angel of Death struck down the firstborn of the Egyptians but then, when he saw the blood of the Israelites, passed over their homes and spared them on the night before the miraculous exodus across the Red Sea.

When our Lord Jesus Christ preached the most famous message of all time—the Sermon on the Mount—He made it plain that He had not come to abolish the Law of Moses, but to fulfill it. In fact, His entire message was based on it; He merely extended its application. And when He had finished, He warned, "Everyone who hears these words of mine and does not put them into practice is like a foolish man who built his house on sand. The rain came down, the streams rose, and the winds blew and beat against that house, and it fell with a great crash" (Matthew 7:26-27) But "everyone who hears these words of mine and puts them into practice is like a wise man who built his house on the rock. The rain came down, the streams rose, and the winds blew and beat against that house; yet it did not fall, because it had its foundation on the rock" (Matthew 7:23-25).

The rock, of course, is Christ—but remember that He is Jesus, the Jew, the fulfillment of every promise, prophecy, and feast in the Jewish Tenakh (our Old Testament). Christianity didn't come out of the blue; our faith goes back 4,000 years to the faith of Abraham, not just 2,000 as supposed by some. Jesus didn't just fill a spiritual vacuum; He was the fulfillment of thousands of years of expectation. To Christians in Rome who in their arrogance seemed to dismiss the Hebraic background to their faith, St. Paul thundered, "You do not support the root, but the root supports you" (Romans 11:18).

As an unfortunate precedent for the current wave of "replacement theology," the Afrikaners of South Africa (from whom I am descended myself) built on a wrong foundation when they created the policy of apartheid on the basis of a Biblical passage (Joshua 9, about how the Gibeonites became servants of the Israelites) that they misinterpreted. But almost as soon as they corporately acknowledged that they had misread and misapplied the Scriptures, the entire structure of apartheid collapsed.

I trust and pray that a similar breakthrough will occur when those advocating "replacement theology" repent of their anti-Semitism and unbelief.

And it's worth noting that former Spanish Prime Minister Jose Maria Aznar has urged support for Israel on the basis that "if it goes down, we all go down."[2] He argues that the Jewish state is at the cutting edge in the battle between militant Islam and the West and, in a *Times* article, concludes, "Israel is a fundamental part of the West which is what it is thanks to its Judeo-Christian roots. If the Jewish element of those roots is upturned and Israel lost, then we are lost too. Whether we like it or not our fate is inextricably intertwined."[3]

---

2 Jose Maria Aznar, "Support Israel: if it goes down, we all go down," *The London Times,* June 17, 2010, http://www.thetimes. co.uk/tto/opinion/columnists/article2559280.ece

3 Ibid.

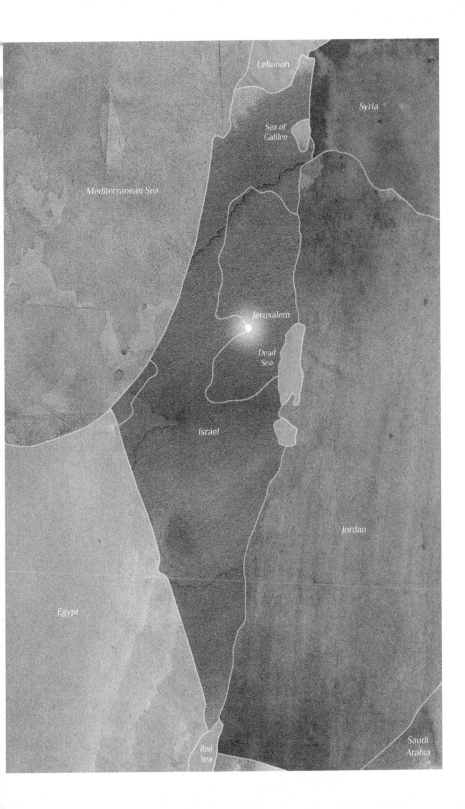

Bibliography

BOOKS

Crombie, Kelvin, *Restoring Israel: 200 Years of the CMJ Story*, Nicolayson's, Ltd, Christ Church, Jerusalem, 2008.

Davis, David, *The Road to Carmel*, published by David Davis, Haifa, Israel, 1997 (previously published by Destiny Image as *Valley of Trouble, Mountain of Hope*).

Guinness, Michele, *Woman —The Full Story: A Dynamic Celebration of Freedoms*, Zondervan, Grand Rapids, Michigan, 2003.

Khaldi, Ishmael, *A Shepherd's Journey: The story of Israel's first Bedouin diplomat*, published by Ishmael Khaldi, Israel, 2010.

Koenig, William R., *Eye to Eye: Facing the Consequences of Dividing Israel*, About Him Publisher, 2008

McTernan, John P., PhD, *As America Has Done to Israel*, Whitaker House, New Kensington, Pennsylvania, 2008.

Netanyahu, Benjamin, *A Durable Peace – Israel and its place among the nations*, Grand Central Publishing (formerly Warner Books) 2000 (first published 1993) grandcentralpublishing.com

Ponsonby, Simon, *God Is for Us, 52 Readings from Romans*, Monarch Books (an imprint of Lion Hudson), Oxford, England, 2013.

Ryle, J. C., *Are You Ready For The End Of Time?* Fearn, Scotland: Christian Focus, 2001; reprint of *Coming Events and Present Duties*.

Saada, Tass with Merrill, Dean, *Once an Arafat Man*, Tyndale House Publishers, Illinois, 2008.

Smith, Lynley, *From Matron to Martyr*, Tate Publishing, USA, 2012.

Thatcher, Margaret, *Margaret Thatcher – The Autobiography*, Harper Perennial, New York, 2013.

Wilson, Marvin R., *Our Father Abraham: Jewish Roots of the Christian Faith*, Wm. B. Eerdmans Publishing Company, Grand Rapids, MI, 1990.

ARTICLES

Aznar, Jose Maria, "Support Israel: if it goes down, we all go down," *The London Times*, June 17, 2010, http://www.the-times.co.uk/tto/opinion/columnists/article2559280.ece

Grider, Geoffrey, "12 SHOCKING PROOFS THAT DISAS-TER STRIKES AMERICA WHEN IT MISTREATS ISRAEL," July 22, 2014, *Now The End Begins*, www.nowth-eendbegins.com, http://www.nowtheendbegins.com/blog/?p=22211, accessed Mar. 2015.

Gutfreund, Sara Debbie, "A Tribute to Margaret Thatcher," *aish.com Your Life*. *Your Judaism*. aish.com, April 8 2013, http://www.aish.com/ci/s/A-Tribute-to-Margaret-Thatcher.html, accessed Mar. 2015.

Hill, Dr. Clifford, "Storms Over Britain, Who's to Blame?" *Christians Together in the Highlands and Islands* online magazine, www.christianstogether.net, Feb. 2014, http://www.christianstogether.net/Articles/393253/Christians_Together_in/Christian_Life/Is_there_any/Storms_over_Britain.aspx, accessed Mar. 2015.

Kendal, Elizabeth, "SYRIA: Who is deploying chemical weapons?" Christian Press, christianpress.com, Sept. 5, 2013, reprinted from *ASSIST News Service*, http://www.christianpress.com/world/851-syria-who-is-deploying-chemical-weapons.html, accessed, April 2015.

Kendal, "Sudan: Khartoum's rulings are totally consistent with Islam," *Christian Liberty Monitoring*, May 20, 2014, http://elizabethkendal.blogspot.com/2014/05/sudan-khartoums-rulings-are-totally.html, accessed, April 2015.

Kitson, Hugh, "Blessings and Curses in a Snowy Jerusalem," *In Touch*, cfi.org.uk/intouch.php, Quarter 1, 2014, http://www.cfi.org.uk/intouch.php?issue=47, accessed Mar. 2015.

Lazarus, David, "Jesus Goes to Auschwitz in Jews For Jesus Film," *Israel Today*, April 27, 2014, http://www.israeltoday.co.il/NewsItem/tabid/178/nid/24575/Default.aspx?article=related_stories

ARTICLES (cont.)

Lawson, Dominic, "So who still thinks Israel is the root of Middle East problems?" *The Independent,* Sept, 2, 2013, http://www.independent.co.uk/voices/comment/dominic-lawson-so-who-still-thinks-israel-is-the-root-of-middle-east-problems-8794664.html, accessed Apr. 2015.

Perlman, Susan interview, "Jesus Goes to Auschwitz in Jews For Jesus Film" by David Lazarus, *Israel Today,* April 27, 2014, http://www.israeltoday.co.il/NewsItem/tabid/178/nid/24575/Default.aspx?article=related_stories, accessed Jan. 2015.

Phillips, Melanie, "A church of hate: An open letter to the Archbishop of Canterbury, Justin Welby," *Melanie Phillips Electric Media Blog,* Dec. 28, 2013, https://www.embooks.com/blog/single/a-church-of-hate, accessed Jan. 2015.

Phillips, Melanie, "It's 1938 all over again," *Melanie Phillips Electric Media Blog,* Nov. 22, 2013, https://www.embooks.com/blog/single/its-1938-all-over-again, accessed, April 2015.

Rosenberg, Bernhard, "Holocaust Remembrance Day: 'That Jew Died for You' is Film of Compassion," *The Christian Post,* April 28, 2014, http://www.christianpost.com/news/holocaust-remembrance-day-that-jew-died-for-you-is-film-of-compassion-118703/#wjz2wiglHEheB1jk.99

Schneider, Aviel, "The Rabbi, the Note and the Messiah," *Israel Today,* May 30, 2013, reprint of cover story, April 2007 issue of *Israel Today Magazine,* http://www.israeltoday.co.il/NewsItem/tabid/178/nid/23877, accessed, April 2015.

NEWSPAPERS, MAGAZINES, BLOGS, etc.

ASSIST News Service, (Aid to Special Saints in Strategic Times), Lake Forest, California

At the Crossroads website, https://middleeastcrossroads.wordpress.com/

CMJ Australia http://cmjaustralia.server101.com/ministries.shtml

Newspapers, Magazines, Blogs, (cont.)

CMJ Israel http://www.cmj-israel.org/dnn/AboutCMJ

CMJ South Africa http://www.cmj-sa.org/

CMJ UK http://www.cmj.org.uk/

CMJ USA http://www.cmj-usa.org

Charisma magazine, Lake Mary, Florida, www.charismamag.com

Christianity Today, magazine, started by Billy Graham, Carol Stream, Illinois, www.christianitytoday.com

In Touch quarterly magazine, Christian Friends of Israel, Jerusalem, http://www.cfi.org.uk/intouch.php

Israel Today, magazine, Jerusalem, israeltoday.co.il

Jerusalem Post newspaper, Jerusalem, jpost.com

Kendal, Elizabeth, *Religious Liberty Monitoring* blog, elizabethkendal. blogspot.com

Phillips, Melanie, *Melanie Phillips Electric Media Blog*, embooks.com/ blog

Phillips, Melanie, *Melanie Phillips Journalist*, Community Facebook page, https://www.facebook.com/MelanieLatest?pnref= story

Soakell, David, editor, *Watching Over Zion*, newsletter, Christian Friends of Israel, Jerusalem, https://www.cfi.org.uk/ watching-over-zion.html

The Foundation for Relief and Reconciliation in the Middle East, Vicar Andrew White's St. George's Church, Baghdad, frrme.org

Wienecke, Rick, *The Fountain of Tears*, sculpture, http://www.casting seeds.com/fountain.html (video) (The DVD, which is longer than this video, can be purchased on this website.)

Wilson, Marvin R., "How Judaism Helped Me to Understand My Bible," interview, (video), YouTube.com, July 17, 2012, https://www.youtube.com/watch?v=C60wlGk2wTg

ARTICLES on *The Crossroads* by Gardner

Listed in order of date published.
(Copyrights by Charles Gardner. All rights reserved.)

April 9, 2014, "Iranian to embrace Jews in Israel," *Heart of Sussex,* online newspaper, http://www.heartpublications.co.uk/iranian-to-embrace-jews-in-israel/, accessed Jan. 2015.

May 12, 2014 "Peace in Our Time - in Jerusalem!" *Israel Today,* Jerusalem, www.israeltoday.co.il, http://www.israeltoday.co.il/Default.aspx?tabid=178&nid=24602, accessed April 2015.

May 12, 2014 "Peace in Our Time - in Jerusalem!" *Encounter Gospel News,* http://encountergospelnews.blogspot.com/2014/05/peace-in-our-time-in-jerusalem.html, accessed April 2015.

May 14 2014, "Where the Cross of Christ Unites Jew and Arab" (same article as above with a different title), *Gateway News,* South Africa, gatewaynews.co.za/Where-the-cross-of-Christ-unites-Jew-and-Arab/, accessed Jan. 2015.

May 14 2014, "Muslim Goes to Mecca—and Finds Jesus," *Gateway News,* South Africa, gatewaynews.co.za/Muslim-goes-to-Mecca-and-finds-Jesus/, accessed Jan. 2015.

May 15, 2014, "Muslim Goes to Mecca—and Finds Jesus!" *Israel Today,* www.israeltoday.co.il, http://www.israeltoday.co.il/NewsItem/tabid/178/nid/24612/Default.aspx?archive=article_title, accessed Jan. 2015.

May 16 2014, "Israel and Iran Pray for Each Other," *Gateway News,* South Africa, gatewaynews.co.za/Israel-and-Iran-pray-for-each-other/, accessed Jan. 2015.

May 16, 2014, "Muslim Finds Jesus During Pilgrimage to Mecca," *WND* (formerly *World Net Daily*), http://www.wnd.com/2014/05/muslim-finds-jesus-during-pilgrimage-to-mecca/, accessed Jan. 2015.

May 18, 2014, "Israel and Iran Pray for Each Other," *Israel Today,* Jerusalem, www.israeltoday.co.il, http://www.israeltoday.co.il/NewsItem/tabid/178/nid/24616/Default.aspx?archive=article_title, accessed Jan. 2015.

ARTICLES on *The Crossroads* (cont.)

May 19, 2014, "From Baghdad to Jerusalem," *Israel Today*, Jerusalem, www.israeltoday.co.il, http://www.israeltoday.co.il/NewsItem/tabid/178/nid/24620/Default.aspx?archive=article_title, accessed Jan. 2015.

May 19, 2014, "Vicar of Baghdad Reminds of Iraq's Godly Heritage," *At the Crossroads* website, https://middleeastcrossroads.wordpress.com/2014/05/19/vicar-of-baghdad-reminds-of-iraqs-godly-heritage, accessed Jan. 2015.

May 21, 2014, "Israel and Iran pray for each other, Jerusalem conference witnesses profound gesture of peace" *At the Crossroads* website, https://middleeastcrossroads.wordpress.com/2014/05/21/israel-and-iran-pray-for-each-other/, accessed Jan. 2015.

May 21, 2014, "Petkash: 'We have a very important ministry- to reconcile the world'" *At the Crossroads* website, https://middleeastcrossroads.wordpress.com/2014/05/21/petkash-we-have-a-very-important-ministry-to-reconcile-the-world/, accessed Jan. 2015.

May 22, 2014 "Iranian Woman Shares Journey of Faith in Jerusalem," *Israel Today*, Jerusalem, www.israeltoday.co.il, http://www.israeltoday.co.il/NewsItem/tabid/178/nid/24629/Default.aspx?topic=article_title, accessed Jan. 2015.

May 22, 2014, "Jesus reconciles Iranian couple, Now they serve God together in UK church," *At the Crossroads* website, https://middleeastcrossroads.wordpress.com/2014/05/22/jesus-reconciles-iranian-couple/, accessed Jan. 2015.

May 22 2014, "Jesus Reconciles Muslim Couple," *Gateway News*, South Africa, gatewaynews.co.za/Jesus-reconciles-Muslim-couple/, accessed Jan. 2015.

May 22, 2014, "Is the church ready for a Mid-East awakening?" *At the Crossroads* website, https://middleeastcrossroads.wordpress.com/2014/05/22/is-the-church-ready-for-a-mid-east-awakening/

May 22 2014, "Open Mic Night in Jerusalem," *Gateway News*, South Africa, gatewaynews.co.za/Open-mic-night-in-Jerusalem/, accessed Jan. 2015.

Articles on *The Crossroads* by
Charles Gardner (cont.)

May 25, 2014, "Glory of God is coming from East, says Singapore pastor, A highway to welcome Jesus back!" *At the Crossroads* website, https://middleeastcrossroads.wordpress.com/2014/05/25/glory-of-god-is-coming-from-east-says-singapore-pastor/, accessed Jan. 2015.

June 2, 2014, "Muslim Goes to Mecca – and Finds Jesus!" *Heart of Sussex,* online newspaper, England, http://www.heartpublications.co.uk/muslim-goes-to-mecca-and-finds-jesus/, accessed Jan. 2015.

June 3, 2014, "AMAZING STORIES OF TRANSFORMATION – 'A foretaste of heaven' as Arab and Jew embrace in Jerusalem," *Heart of Sussex,* online newspaper, England, http://www.heartpublications.co.uk/amazing-stories-of-transformation-a-foretaste-of-heaven-as-arab-and-jew-embrace-in-jerusalem/, accessed Jan. 2015. [Also published in their June/July print issue as a major feature (with photos) spread across two-and-a-half pages.]

July 2014, "Arab and Jew embrace in Jerusalem" *Joy!* magazine, South Africa. Specially commissioned 4-page feature spread with photos. (Said to be the biggest Christian publication outside the USA.)

December 2014, "Turkish delight! Man's Mecca Pilgrimage Ends in Conversion Shock," *New Life* newspaper, (main front page piece), http://issuu.com/newlifepublishing/docs/nl250_dec2014

For videos and audios from the *At The Crossroads* meetings and more articles about it, go to to their website: https://middleeastcrossroads.wordpress.com/2014/05/

Other Articles by Charles Gardner

"Charles Gardner" author profile page with a list of his many articles, *Blirt Magazine*, www.blirt-magazine.com, http://www.blirt-magazine.com/profile/?id=439, accessed Jan. 2015, but no longer accessible since Feb 2015.*

Jan. 20, 2015, "The blessing of Jewish heritage," *The Times of Israel*, blogs.timesofisrael.com, http://blogs.timesofisrael.com/the-blessing-of-jewish-heritage/

Jan. 26, 2015, "A brave Scot's Auschwitz horror," *The Times of Israel*, blogs.timesofisrael.com, http://blogs.timesofisrael.com/a-brave-scots-auschwitz-horror/

Feb. 3, 2015, "Evangelical Christians—consistent friends of Israel!" *The Times of Israel*, blogs.timesofisrael.com, http://blogs.timesofisrael.com/evangelical-christians-consistent-friends-of-israel/

Feb. 11, 2015, "Hear O Israel: God is speaking!" *The Times of Israel*, blogs.timesofisrael.com, http://blogs.timesofisrael.com/hear-o-israel-god-is-speaking/

Mar. 22, 2015, "No peace for the wicked," *The Times of Israel*, blogs.timesofisrael.com, http://blogs.timesofisrael.com/no-peace-for-the-wicked/

See more of his articles on *The Times of Israel* at: http://blogs.timesofisrael.com/author/charles-gardner/

Other Books by Charles Gardner

Israel the Chosen: Why the Jews are So Special, Create Space, 2013.

Tongues of Fire: The Phenomenon That Set the World Alight, Sable Publishing, Somerset, England, 2007.

Doctor on the Run: The Memoirs and Prescriptions of Dr David Gardner, Sable Publishing, Somerset, England, 2007.

Publications for which Gardner contributes

ASSIST (Aid to Special Saints In Strategic Times) News Service, a global agency based in California

Blirt Magazine, online magazine, England*

Doncaster Free Press (part of the group from which the author retired two years ago)

Gateway News, South Africa (an online news portal)

Heart of Sussex, print and online newspaper, heartpublications.co.uk

Israel Today, Jerusalem, israeltoday.co.il

Joy! magazine, South Africa

New Life newspaper (an evangelistic tabloid the author founded 33 years ago), England

Good News (a rival outreach paper), England

Prophecy Today (the online re-launch of a very influential Christian voice in the UK), England

The Times of Israel, a global, online newspaper, timesofisrael.com

WND (formerly *World Net Daily*), wnd.com, U.S.

*Publisher's note: *Blirt* magazine and website no longer exists. It has been sold on Flippa.com. (See https://flippa.com/2971606-news-and-blogging-platform-with-475-writers-650-articles-published) Here is what the author says about that:

"Actually I see this as a huge positive because it happened just as I got accepted as a blogger for the *Times of Israel.* It was as if the Lord was opening one door as He was closing another. In fact, it seems He was simply saying that my time was up in spreading the Gospel through that particular *secular* site. I saved most of the original articles and many of them (certainly those about the Middle East) have been incorporated either into my first book on Israel or this one! So it's no loss. Everything is for a season. I've felt a call to enter the heat of the mainstream media debate where they are, rather than always in a 'cozy Christian corner.' And, with approaching 90,000 views for 95 articles over 19 months, I think it proved that there is a hunger out there for real spiritual answers! Hallelujah!"

Peace in Jerusalem

is available at:

olivepresspublisher.com

amazon.com

barnesandnoble.com

christianbook.com

deepershopping.com

parable.com

and other online stores

Store managers:

Order wholesale through:

Ingram Book Company or

Spring Arbor

or by emailing:

olivepressbooks@gmail.com

CPSIA information can be obtained
at www.ICGtesting.com
Printed in the USA
LVOW04s1738260716

497853LV00024B/1025/P